THE SECRET PLACES OF THE WEST CORK COAST

D1249120

THE SECRET PLACES
OF THE
WEST CORK COAST

JOHN M. FEEHAN

ROYAL CARBERY BOOKS

ROYAL CARBERY BOOKS
36 Beechwood Park, Ballinlough, Cork

Trade Distributors:
MERCIER PRESS
PO Box 5, 5 French Church Street, Cork
16 Hume Street, Dublin 2

Trade enquiries to CMD DISTRIBUTION,
55a Spruce Avenue, Stillorgan Industrial Park, Blackrock, Dublin

© The Estate of John M Feehan

ISBN 0 946645 11 6

This book was first published in 1978 and reprinted in 1979 under the title *The Wind that Round the Fastnet Sweeps.* It was first published under the title *The Secret Places of the West Cork Coast* in 1990.

10 9 8 7 6 5 4

Printed in Ireland by Colour Books Ltd.

INTRODUCTION

Black Dan, a wild unruly travelling man from rich pasture lands far from the sea, was taken by surprise when I told him I was going to sail alone the full length of the West Cork coast, almost one hundred miles of water, in a small wooden boat not much longer than his own caravan. 'Was there no passenger ship going that way,' he wanted to know, 'or why for couldn't I get the bus?' Dan had only seen the sea twice in his life and what he saw did not appeal to him. As luck would have it I was with him both times. The first was at Tramore on a wild blustery day in early June when the great waves were pounding on the golden strand and the wind sending cascades of sparkling spray high into the clear summer air. Dan gazed hard and long at what must have been to him a most bewildering and confusing sight, something he had never seen before, and then he turned to me and said:

'By Christ, no matter what the Russians say, there's a God.' He had learned more theology in those few moments than many another in a lifetime at a seminary.

The next time, and the last by his express wish, was at Dungarvan. I had hired a small rowing boat and he nervously sat in the stern trying his best to hide his anxiety and fear. When we passed the calm water sheltered by the pier we met a very slight swell. His face began to turn a kind of grey as if the blood was draining out of it, and I asked him if he was alright but he seemed unable to give a coherent answer. There was no point in causing him further distress so I turned the boat around and rowed back to the pier. We were less than five minutes out and his relief was unbounded. He stepped unsteadily ashore and when I had tied up we made our way along the cobbled quays towards the nearest hostelry. As we were about to enter he turned around and looked at the harbour, the boats, and the slight swell outside. 'By God 'tis great to be back in Ireland again,' he said with a broad grin on his rugged face.

The reaction of Dan to the sea was predictable. It was nothing more than the reaction of thousands of landsmen all over the country; a reaction of fear and mistrust of something they did not know or understand. The men of the land find it hard to understand the men who sail the seas in small boats; but for those of us who want to do this alone we must appear as stark, raving lunatics!

I opted to make this passage from Cork to Crookhaven alone in a small wooden sailing boat. Let me introduce her to you. First of all her name is *Dualla*, called after a little country graveyard in County Tipperary where all that is left of the woman who loved me and shared my life awaits the final hour of the Resurrection. *Dualla* is Bermudian rigged, has a large main sail and a series of smaller foresails. She is thirty-one feet long, eight feet across and draws five feet six inches of water. She can sleep four in reasonable comfort and has all the usual accessories such as toilet, gas cooker, wash up, etc. To push her along when there is no wind or when a strong tide goes contrary at the mouth of a harbour she has a 25 h.p. Volvo diesel engine. A nine foot collapsible rubber punt ferries me backwards and forwards, from wherever she is anchored, to a landing slip or pier. Those are her vital statistics.

Now let me introduce myself. I am a publisher by profession, a writer by inclination, a soldier by training and a man of the sea in the deepest recess of my heart. I am no longer young, indeed I am well beyond the canonical age. I make a special point of this fact for the benefit of the many undoubtedly sincere and well-meaning women who read my last book, *Tomorrow To Be Brave,* and who wrote to me saying that they cried so much when reading it, that I must be a very kind and understanding man, and that it is quite wrong of me to continue to go through life alone without the joys of female companionship. I do not apologise for causing their tears. Tears become a woman very much and are indeed an essential part of her whole personality; besides which I know that to cry bears witness to the greatest courage of all — the courage to understand suffering. I must however disappoint them in the little matter of their other assumption. 'Far off cows have long horns,' says the old Irish proverb, and I can assure them that I am not nearly as nice as they think. If they want evidence of this I refer them to John B. Keane who, in his role as matchmaker, has tried hard over the past six years to remedy this situation only to meet with failure time and time again. In the end he washed his hands completely of me and told me angrily to get to hell back to my cottage on the remote cliffs of Cork harbour, and stay there forever with my dogs, sea-gulls, kittiwakes and corncrakes since they were more fitting company for me than decent human beings. So there you are. You can't win all the time, can you?

The coast of West Cork I know very well. I have sailed .. every summer for at least fifteen years and at one time or another called at each of the many captivating harbours, great and small, which abound on that picturesque and enchanting stretch of shoreline. In those days I always had one or two friends with me to lend a hand; friends with whom I shared the joys of the open sea, the comfort of a snug harbour and warm friendly tavern at the end of a hard days run, friends to whom I have dedicated this book. But now it was going to be different. I was going to sail alone without help or companions. I do not wish to give the impression that I am an anti-social crank with my hand raised against every man, or a snob who thinks his own company more pleasant than that of anybody else. Indeed no. I have a deep affection for all human beings; an affection, I fear, far greater than most of them have for me. But like all others I have my favourites and my prejudices. I cannot say that I have ever been particularly attracted by the high, the mighty or the very rich. I have known quite a lot of them during the run of my life and, behind the veneer of importance which they like to assume, most of them are extraordinarily empty and shallow. Bismark said that during the course of his life he saw three Emperors naked and the sight did not impress him.

I have mostly found that I have a great rapport with those human beings who are just themselves and nothing more, and who do not try by vulgar ostentation or loud talk to be that which they are not. One day, so an old Irish folk-tale goes, the Lord was walking in the Garden of Paradise and he came by a little forget-me-not growing at the foot of a massive oak tree. The little flower spoke to the Lord and said:

'I wish I were like the oak tree here, strong, powerful and majestic. Then I could be of some use to the world.' And the Lord answered: 'If you tried to be an oak you would end up revolting and ugly. Your beauty lies in being what you are — a simple, lovely flower that has brought so much more happiness to the hearts of young lovers than any oak tree. Your simplicity and your loveliness is yourself.' Thus spoke the Lord words of wisdom that have a message for us all whether we sail the seas, or climb the mountains or walk the leafy woodland paths. The most wonderful friends in life are those people who are just themselves; believe me, I know it, I've met hundreds of them and those who came closest were those who shared the perils of the sea.

My decision to make this passage alone was not based on my likes or dislikes of various human beings but it was connected in a very intimate way with the death of the one human being who was supreme in my life. When my wife Mary died I wrote a book called *Tomorrow To Be Brave* which had a twofold purpose; to tell the story of a remarkable and wonderful woman who knew she was going to die but who faced up to it with unbelievable courage and fortitude, and who turned her last terrible years on this earth into the greatest years of her life; and secondly to try to explain what happens to a man when he loses the woman

8

he loves – the insanity that possesses him, the cowardice that besets him, the total darkness that engulfs every corner of his soul. I believe I succeeded in the first purpose and failed in the second. I was too close to it all – the raw gaping wounds of pain and sorrow had not nearly healed. Only now, six years later, can I look upon it with some calmness and common sense, and try to conceive a workable plan to rebuild my life, particularly my inner life, from the ashes and rubble of the past. 'Life is a series of agonies which we can only climb on bruised and aching knees,' cried Amiel. We all experience moments of great richness, moments of deep rewarding intensity, moments of supreme happiness; but they have no permanence. 'Stay O happy moment, stay!' was the agonising cry of Faust. The moment of happiness paves the way for suffering, the moment of suffering paves the way for hope, and the moment of hope prepares us for happiness again, and so round and round it goes in a vicious circle like the endless spinning of a roulette wheel. To help me to bring the threads of my life together again, in some meaningful pattern, was the reason I undertook this cruise alone. I hoped that the long hours at sea without telephone, without letters, without the necessity of having to make conversation would give me ample time to think, to face the enigma of my own self and perhaps to see some path of meaning, not only in the sad happenings of the past, but in the probabilities of the unknown future. When I started out on this cruise I believed that before it ended the silence of the sea would have given me some magic formula that would banish for ever the turmoil which had been my lot for six years. I know that all this will be hard for the ordinary person to understand, but we each have to go our own way, and this was my road in search of myself. 'The heart has its reasons that are unknown to reason,' said Pascal. For those who have suffered the pain of separation through death no explanation is necessary; they will understand every word I write. For those who have not, no explanation may be possible; but I will honestly try my best. No man can do more and with that we must all be satisfied.

J. M. F.
January 1978

1

After a quick lunch at the Yacht Club I left the moorings in Crosshaven one beautiful summer's day very early in July. My first destination was Kinsale which, with the moderate North-West wind then blowing, should not take more than three to four hours. I had spent the forenoon stowing *Dualla* with food, water, diesel, bedding and various other commodities required for a cruise and had listened to the shipping forecast at two o'clock which gave North-Westerly, force three to four, a fair wind which would fill all sails, and blowing off the land ensure that the seas would be calm. This is the yachtsman's dream, but it doesn't often come about and more frequently it blows strong from the South-West, bringing in big surging seas, and then the trip to Kinsale becomes a hard tough beat lasting six or maybe seven hours.

When I turned the corner at Fort Davis and faced the Atlantic the enormity of what I was about to do came suddenly upon me, and I was so filled with fear and depression that I seriously thought of turning back. You can plan something carefully, think about it, yearn and long to do it, but only when you are about to put it into effect does its magnitude strike you. But in the midst of this mood of dejection a gust of wind caught the sails and *Dualla* sprung gallantly to life. Lifting her head like a thorough-bred at the starting line, she tore through the seas, on and on and on, past the coves and strands and heathered rocks, on to the mouth of the harbour and out into the open sea. That little puff of wind banished my depression and it felt great to be alive. By such trifles are we ruled.

The stretch of coastline between Fort Davis and Ringa-bella Bay, which now seemed to be charging past me, like a landscape from the windows of a train, has a strange assortment of bungalows, cottages, shacks and converted railway carriages with such highly original names as *Sea View, Wave Crest, Sunset, Tall Timbers, The Nook, The Haven* etc., each with its own little flower garden, lovingly tended if a retired couple happen to be living there, but overgrown and wild if it was only the week-end retreat of someone who lived in Cork or further away. There is a story told of a very devout woman, albeit a bit of a snob, who built a distinguished and unusual bungalow in these parts. She wanted her bungalow to have an exotic name with a Continental flavour, perhaps French, and some local wag suggested *Le Bordel*. She was delighted. She thought it had an enchanting musical sound and was quite exotic. So she had a renowned stone-cutter etch the name in marble and it was set into the front balustrade. As was the custom Mass was said in the new house and it was blessed by the curate who also thought the name very novel and unique. A few months later a couple of drunken French fishermen whose trawler was sheltering from a storm, hammered noisily on the door and demanded service. Luckily one of them spoke a little English and it was only then the good woman found out that *Le Bordel* in French meant 'whore house' in English. She promptly put the run on the fishermen, renamed the house after a saint and had another Mass said there – this time by the parish priest who used the Latin rite, just to make absolutely certain.

Quite soon I was crossing Ringabella Bay itself and the North-West wind swept down over Fountainstown, struck *Dualla's* already full-blown sails, heeled her over 'til her rails were awash. She was now charging at top speed through the water scattering cascades of silver spray high into the clear air. As I sat there in the cockpit I found the whole scene exciting and almost intoxicating. There was the fresh pure wind whistling all around me, the beautiful soft sound of the waves as they lashed the decks and dissolved into a mass of soothing foam. It was like as if I had woken up in another world and had shaken off the tense life of the city with all

11

its jaded compensations. And there in this exhilarating atmosphere I began to think, rather smugly I fear, of what it would be like in the city as I sailed gaily along on the high seas. In a few hours the surging masses would leave their shops and offices and stream homewards, scurrying almost like frightened beetles from under a stone that you'd turn upside down. There was a fair chance that there would be a greasy supper of tinned beans and chips, accompanied by a white pasty thing called bread; then an hour or so snoring by the fire, sourly waking up to look at T.V. and then ending the last hours of the day in some suffocating chromium-plated pub with a jukebox and pool table. Great God! How terrible for me, but how happy for those who want that, and who have indeed a right to it. All our values are relative as I once learned long years ago not far inland from where I was now sailing. A friend of mine, who was a labouring man, became invalided and could work no more. He lived in a small cottage by the side of the road with no running water or electric light. Worse still the wife he loved ran away to England with a local carpenter and left him to support their two children, Mick aged twelve and Joe aged nine, on a miserable weekly pittance being paid in Home Assistance. I believe they were, like so many of the sick poor, virtually on the starvation line. One day many summers ago I brought the two young boys, neither of whom had ever seen the sea, for an outing to beautiful Garrettstown strand. We sat together on the rocks enjoying the breathtaking scene before us. It was one of those perfect days when everything was right. A soft gentle wind was blowing inwards from the Atlantic; the birds were gliding with grace and beauty through the air; the sea was a Mediterranean blue. Everything was radiant and the world was mine. I gazed out to the horizon and partly in a reverie I spoke out loud:

'My God! This is like Heaven.'

There was no reply. Then a strange impulse got hold of me and I turned to Mick, the twelve-year-old, and said:

'Mick. What's your idea of Heaven?'

The answer came without hesitation.

'Heaven,' he said in a quiet voice, 'is a place where you'd never be hungry.' We all have our priorities; for some it is caviar and champagne; others must be satisfied with less.

I now set *Dualla* on to self-steering and went down below to brew a decent mug of tea — a reflex action from my army days. I had first of all scanned the surface in a wide circle with the field glasses in case there were any salmon nets on my course but I could pick out no buoys and it looked as if everything were clear. These salmon nets can be a nuisance, especially if they get entangled in the propeller, and I've cursed them many times, but then again the salmon men have to live as well as the rest of us and we can't be too hard on them. I came back on deck again with a steaming mug in my hands and sat down at my ease in the cockpit to enjoy it all. Those little electronic steering devices are a marvellous help and they can keep the boat on course in all but the most violent conditions. Cork by any standards is a very beautiful county but Cork from the sea is really awe-inspiring. The sailor sees the cliffs and the coast from the opposite side to the landsman who looks down and out, while the sailor looks in and up and he views those lofty sublime precipices, deeply indented with caves where the seals make their homes and where the restless Atlantic waves lash back and forth and in and out from day to day, week to week, year to year and century to century. The face of Ireland has changed a lot down the centuries but the coastline has remained the same. What I was now looking at and admiring was exactly what our ancestors, those tall, fair and warlike figures, saw when they came from the east, through France and Spain, and northern Europe to land in their small, frail boats on our desolate shores more than five thousand years ago. They were in the main farmers and hunters and they came to this strange uninhabited island to make a new life, to plough and sow, to reap and bind, to hunt and chase, to love and marry and to father a race of proud people, later to be known as Irishmen. And I was looking at the same cliffs, the same unpretentious hills they saw when they sailed over the horizon in that far away and distant past.

One by one I passed the little bays and the tall headlands whose names always arouse my curiosity. How did Man-of-War Cove get its name? Was this where a man-of-war was wrecked or was it a smugglers' look-out? How did New-foundland Bay get its name? Which came first — it or its namesake across the Atlantic? Whom does Jordan Bay commemorate? Was there once a family of landlords powerful enough to have a bay called after them? Cork Head, Roberts Head, Reanies Head, Flat Head, Barrys Head, one by one I left them all behind me. Not far off from my port side I passed the dangerous submerged Daunt's Rock called after Achilles Daunt, High Sheriff of Cork, who arrested a dis-possessed Irish farmer turned bucaneer called Philip Og Barry at Roberts Cove. But the farmer was one step ahead of the King's messenger and he turned the tables on Daunt, weighed him with irons and sank him to the bottom of the rock. The rock was called after Daunt and one of the head-lands after Barry, who was never again apprehended and died in his bed at a ripe old age.

I soon found myself sailing between the two majestic Sovereign Rocks at the entrance to Oyster Haven harbour. No matter what happens now, I thought, I'm safe. Even if it blew a hurricane I could always slip into Oyster Haven which is one of the loveliest and most delightful anchorages on the south coast. I remember once in a pub in Kinsale an old fisherman telling me the story of a famous rescue that took place just off the Sovereigns which I was passing. In Novem-ber 1818 a ship called *The Sylvan* struck the big Sovereign Rock in a gale of particularly violent force, and with the exception of one young child, who managed to scramble onto the rock, everyone else was lost. For two days and two nights the young child clung on, crying helplessly, while coastguards and English naval vessels circled around afraid to make any attempt at rescue. This was left to the heroism of a simple Irish fisherman, Jack Carty, who tied a rope around his body, and with one end made fast to his boat, swam through the mountainous seas and brought the half-dead child to safety, while all the power of the English navy looked stupidly on.

'Jack-the-Rock, as he was afterwards called, was a near kinsman of my own,' the fisherman told me. 'He got no medal or piece of paper, but there are old men living still in Oyster Haven, who will tell you that story as they heard it from their grandfathers. But sure I suppose 'tis better to be talked of around the Irish firesides for a hundred years than any medal.'

I was now beginning to feel quite cocky because I had almost reached my first day's destination on my first sail alone, and although it was only a matter of a few hours, for me, it was a fulfilling achievement. I had been sailing for twenty years but I had never sailed alone. I suppose it was this thought that put me in mind of the man who aroused my interest in the sea and planted in my soul a curiosity as restless as the waves themselves, and also the fact that a few miles due south from where I was, a drama was enacted with this man that would be hard to equal even in the annals of the most imaginative fiction. Let me tell you this story.

He was known to all as Captain Albert (out of my love for him I will withhold his real name). He came from England to retire, as he said, from a lifetime of the captaincy of ships, and he took house with an attractive and much younger woman on a beautiful site overlooking Cork harbour. It would not have been easy to find two people more contrasting in every way. She, whose name was Betsy, was at least twenty years younger, quiet, gentle, dignified and almost regal in her tall and lithesome body. He was short, boisterous, wild, with a vocabulary of Rabelaisian language, that would have put any drunken British Tommy to shame. Many long winter nights I sat with him before a blazing log fire and listened to his captivating stories of the sea. He was trained in the days of sail on one of those great three-masters that circumnavigated the world in hurricanes, storms and calms. He was twice wrecked off Cape Horn and managed to survive. Later during Prohibition days he illegally ran liquor down the St Lawrence river in Canada into the ports on the east coast of the United States. Here he was attacked by real present-day pirates who machine-gunned his ship and fought a life and death struggle for the valuable alcoholic prizes on board. He had an encyclopaedic knowledge of all the principal harbours of the world, and without pausing he could describe in detail the leading lights, the buoys, the water-depths in any major harbour you might care to ask him about. He knew the haunts of sailing men in these harbours; where every little item of personal requirement could be bought and its price. He had a special knowledge of whores and whore houses but since I am writing this book for pure joy and not as a contribution to modern English literature, I will omit the details which he described with gusto and relish. His study was a museum in miniature. Along one wall was an extensive and valuable library of books on shipping, navigation, stowage, sailing directions and many other aspects of sea-faring life. The other walls were decorated with mementos from every ship he had sailed on; ship-lamps, lifebelts, a compass, a sextant, a sea log, a wheel, the flags of all his ships and several other items that go with the ways of the sea. Dominating the entire room, like a Father-God figure, was a large portrait in oils of himself in the uniform of a Merchant Navy Captain, and printed in old English script on the golden frame was Masefield's beautiful couplet:

> *I must go down to the sea again,*
> *To the lonely sea and the sky. . .*

Here he passed his days in quiet retirement, sometimes gazing longingly out to sea, surrounded by the memories of the world of the past and the men he loved. And it was in this very atmosphere, and under his charismatic spell that I too, longingly awaited the day when I could become, like him, one of the men who go down to the sea. He planned that when summer came, he would take me in hand, and teach me the art of handling a small boat. But no man can be certain of anything in this world – except his own death, and one cold winter evening when I called to his house after a long absence I found Betsy in tears. Albert had been taken ill suddenly and removed to hospital and at this very moment when I wanted to see him most I was called away on one of those cursed business trips that are the plague of this demanding world, and it was not until three days later that I returned home. When I got to the hospital he was fading rapidly. The end was almost at hand. Betsy and a nun were at his bedside, Betsy crying and the nun standing in an attitude of reverence and awe. He was sleeping uneasily. For a short while no one spoke. Then he opened his eyes slowly and looked first at Betsy and then, rather in bewilderment at me. In a weak faltering voice he said: 'The sea has been my life. I could not bear to be buried in the earth. Promise to bury me at sea... promise...' His eyes closed and his voice trailed away to an inaudible whisper. His face contorted a little as if he wanted to speak again but nothing came except a strange gurgling sound from his throat. For a while he waved his hands wildly but in a few seconds all was quiet. The breathing had stopped and the nun gently pulled the bedclothes over his head.

It was my first sea burial and I shall never attend one again. The coffin was rested on the stern of a fishing trawler and it was decorated with the flags of all his ships taken from his study. A few wreaths of laurels and lily-of-the-valley lay on the top, fluttering in the breeze. It was a calm, still morning; the sun glistened on the sea as we steamed out to his last resting place beyond the three mile limit. Apart from the crew—three fishermen—there were six or seven people on board, all near friends, and a clergyman. Betsy was dressed in black, her red bloodshot eyes temporarily marring her beauty. We made the sad journey in silence, talking only when necessary and in subdued tones. When we arrived at the burial spot the trawler stopped and the fishermen removed their headgear and respectfully crossed themselves. In a moving homily the clergyman said that God in his infinite love and wisdom had seen fit to bring this life, so full of adventure and valour, to a close. Captain Albert's life shone as an example, he said, of that supreme courage and bravery of all mortals whose task it is to go down to the sea in ships. He had traversed the oceans of the world in storm and calm and had faced death with Christian fortitude many times. It was now fitting that he should have died amongst those he loved and that the sea to which he had given the best years of his life should finally receive his mortal remains for all eternity. He ended by quoting Walt Whitman's beautiful poem:

Joy, shipmate, joy;
Pleased to my soul at death I cry
My life is closed, my life begins,
The long, long anchorage I leave,
My ship is clear at last, she leaps!

As the fishermen gently lowered the weighted coffin into the sea the clergyman opened his book and recited that inspiring psalm *Go forth in peace, O Christian Soul.* The coffin floated a little while and then slowly sank. Only the wreaths remained on the surface, buffeting the waves as if possessed by a living spirit. When the prayers were ended the fishermen crossed themselves again, started the engines and headed in for port. I stood alone on the stern watching the wreaths slowly fade out of sight, my mind occupied with awesome thoughts on the savagery of death. It was then Betsy came up to me and spoke quietly. 'I am glad you are here at this moment,' she said. 'You were his best friend in Ireland. He loved you as a son. I think I would be failing in my duty to Albert and to you if I were not to tell you the whole truth, for only now can it be told.' She paused for a moment and looked wistfully back out to sea. 'Poor Albert was certified insane when he lived in London in the early twenties. He was never a sea captain and was never at sea in his life. All his vast knowledge of the sea he learned from a lifetime studying books. The mementos and flags which decorated his room, and just now his coffin, were bought at auctions. He had his portrait painted in a

18

sea-captain's uniform hired from a Theatrical Agency. The only time he was ever at sea was when, a few years ago, we crossed from England to live over here. When the ship left Fishguard his eyes rolled wildly, his body contorted and he fell into a coma out of which he did not emerge until we were securely tied up twelve hours later at Cork jetties. He had an excellent income from family investments and we lived comfortably. I know you will understand all I say to you and that you will not think any the worse of poor Albert. He was insane, harmlessly insane, and he could not help it. Schizophrenia the doctors called it. That was why we never got married. Isn't it strange that only in death could he come to terms with the sea he loved, and which terrorised him so much in life.'

She sat down on an upturned fish-barrel, the tears falling slowly from her eyes. I put my arm around her and rested her head on my shoulder. I did not know whether to laugh or to cry. I tried to pray but the words stuck in my throat. In the distance, over the tops of the waves, I could still faintly see the lily-of-the-valley bobbing up and down. For a brief moment I felt I could hear Albert's boisterous laughter coming from the depths. Indeed I was not far from laughing myself at the incredible farce we had just enacted. God, in his infinite sense of humour, could hardly have looked too seriously at the whole performance either, for did he not put into the mouth of his psalmist, in the Old Testament, the inspired words: 'I said in my haste: all men are liars.' (Psalm 116:11).

Or was it a farce? Albert lived a joyful, contented and fulfilled life with the woman he loved. His memories were magnificent might-have-beens. He hurt nobody, did injury to nobody. On the contrary, he brought quite a degree of happiness to those he came in contact with, and human beings felt all the better for having known him. In the end he was most mercifully united to that element in nature he feared most, absorbed, at his own request, in a final act of identity with the only enemy he had ever known — the sea. What more can any man reasonably search for — in life or in death?

I could now hear in the distance the whistling buoy which marks the dangerous Bulman Rock at the entrance to Kinsale Harbour. I do not know why this is called a whistling buoy since the sound it emits is more like the wail of a banshee on a winter's night, eerie and spine-chilling, a sound muffled and sad that spoke of wrecks and sea disasters. I took the passage inside the rock and as I passed between Strookaun and Prehaun points I started the engine, set the self steering again, busied myself taking down the sails and making ready the anchor as *Dualla* made her own way towards the town of Kinsale. The water in the harbour itself is too deep and requires too much chain, besides it is uncomfortable from the wash of all the motor boats constantly coming and going, so I continued on past the pier and up into the Bandon river. There in two fathoms of water I dropped the anchor in a safe and comfortable berth. I had completed my first passage alone. I felt as if I were an Irish Chichester!

Later that evening I rowed ashore in the rubber punt feeling happy and at peace with the world mainly, I would say, the result of a satisfying dinner and a delightful Rhine wine. Kinsale is not one of those places I have fallen in love with. It reminds me of a worn-out old whore trying to regain her lost glory and passion. The new rich have moved in because somebody equally as empty as themselves told them that it was the 'thing' to own a Kinsale property. I avoided the fashionable places where they congregate and went to a good Irish pub, crowded I am glad to say with hardy West Cork men, whose conversation was intelligent and whose delightful lilting accents added a note of appropriate background music to the whole scene. When I lied to Mine Host that I was a tourist from the county Leitrim and was never before in Kinsale he dropped his defences and expanded at length about the jet age that had hit his little seaside port.

'Kinsale,' he confided with a knowing wink, 'is the devil's own town. Do you know what they say about us in other parts of the county? They say, "Are you happily married or do you live in Kinsale?" Isn't that a good one? And I'll tell you one better. There was a poet, a class of a Yeats, who came here one summer and wrote a verse of poetry about us:

> The historic old town of Kinsale
> Where they sing as they wash down their ale
> Where each man despite strife
> Lives with his own wife
> If you've heard something else 'tis a tale!

Isn't that a good one for you? There's plenty of randy heifers in Kinsale,' he continued, 'and no shortage of bulls either, young or old as you want them. Would you believe it,' he dropped to a whisper, 'I was out snaring rabbits at six o'clock one morning about a week ago and what do you think I saw but an ould fellow with a pot-belly hanging down to his knees rolling around in the dewy grass with a young one hardly seventeen and not a stitch of clothes on either of them — there's for you now — and we having two chapels, a convent and ten priests in the town!'

'A bloody disgrace,' I answered with my tongue in my cheek. 'A Mass should have been read in the field.'

'Excuse me a minute,' he said as he moved to the other end of the counter to settle some argument between two drunken farmers who looked as if they were going to come to blows.

'Every word of that is true,' said a voice from beside me — a well dressed man in his mid-forties, slightly tipsy who had obviously been evesdropping on our conversation. 'I know all about that side of life and a lot more,' he said. 'I have a very good job in Dublin — I'm a commercial traveller — and have three week's holidays every year. I spend two of them in West Cork going from caravan site to caravan site pretending I'm from the Tourist Board. Whenever I see a likely looking bit, or two, on their own in a caravan I intro-

21

duce myself and welcome them on behalf of the Irish Government. This breaks the ice and before the night is out I have one or the other of them, and if my luck is in I might have the two. Kinsale never failed me yet.' He finished his drink. 'I must be on my way over to the site,' he said. 'I have to go home tomorrow. You see on the last week of my holidays I bring the wife and kids on a bit of a pilgrimage. We're off to Lourdes the day after tomorrow and they'll love it.'

We parted company at the door — he to his last little flutter before experiencing the spiritual joys of Lourdes — I to the aloneness of *Dualla*. As I rowed across the harbour I could see the lights of the caravan site in the distance. I must confess I was tempted, but I realised that dressed as I was in dirty jeans and a torn sweater, no woman, however lonely, would believe I was a senior Government official on a good-will tour of caravan sites.

I made a final check of everything on deck, and went down below to a comfortable bunk to sleep soundly 'til morning.

I stayed four days in Kinsale. The wind swung fiercely into the South-West and I had no mind to spend eight or ten long hours belting into high seas before I reached Glandore or Castlehaven. Far better to stay put in a snug harbour and wait for a fine day and a fair wind. I had plenty to occupy my time in Kinsale. With Michael Mulcahy's *A Short History of Kinsale* I explored the ground of the Battle of Kinsale which is one of those great enigmas of Irish history and which, even to this day, holds the imagination of the public.

The Battle of Kinsale was the Culloden, the Waterloo of Ireland. To every Irishman the word 'Kinsale' means one thing — defeat and disaster, for it was here in 1601 that the old Irish world was broken in its last stand against the foreign invader. The Battle of Kinsale confirmed for three centuries the mighty power of England in Ireland — a power which almost turned us into animals and slaves and which was to send millions of our people to death and destruction before it was finally routed.

Kinsale is a completely puzzling affair and I have never yet come across a satisfactory explanation of the Irish defeat. Why did O'Neill fail to display those brilliant military traits which everyone had come to expect from him? Why after the skirmish — it was not a battle — did he not rally his men and make a second attempt instead of retreating home to the far north of Ireland with his army virtually intact? This is one of the great 'why's' of Irish history. Sean O'Faolain in his book *The Great O'Neill* aptly remarks, 'Mountjoy did not win the battle of Kinsale — O'Neill lost it'. In 1601 O'Neill and his colleague O'Donnell were virtual masters in the north and in the west and in a series of battles, The Yellow Ford, Clontibret, The Curlew Moutains, they had outwitted and defeated the cream of the English generalship, and had raised the hopes of the faltering Irish that a free and united Ireland was at last in sight. O'Neill was a wise and experienced general, and expert strategist, cautious and careful, and never gave battle unless it was absolutely unavoidable. O'Donnell on the other hand was fiery and impulsive, a fine tactician, unquestionably brave, with plenty of imagination and resourcefulness. Despite O'Neill's victories it was clear to him that he could not, alone, banish the English from Ireland. He needed the help of the other Irish chieftains whose loyalty was at best questionable for so long as he could produce victories they were with him, but in the absence of a final rout of the English they kept waiting and watching, fortified by promises of rich lands and honours if they sided against O'Neill. He had no illusion about his fellow countrymen and it was this clear grasp of the realities of the situation that led him to seek the help of England's mortal enemy, Philip of Spain. Philip saw the advantages of helping O'Neill. A united and friendly Ireland would give him an excellent base from which to commence operations against England and ultimately invade, and with this in mind he prepared an Expeditionary Force for Ireland. All this plan was couched in

the most high sounding phrases. It was all to be done to pre-
serve the most glorious Catholic religion from the clutches
of English Protestantism, but in reality neither Philip nor
O'Neill worried too much about religion. Spain's advantage
was uppermost in Philip's mind, and Ireland's freedom in
O'Neill's.

The English commander in the field was Lord Mountjoy,
an able, ruthless general who in the field was no match for
O'Neill, but he had behind him the power of a growing
empire which O'Neill lacked. He, too, knew of the negotiations with Spain and he also realised that the moment a
Spanish army landed in the north all the wavering Irish
chieftains would rally to O'Neill and only a miracle could
save the English power in Ireland. But that miracle happened. Instead of landing in friendly territory in the north
where they could have joined forces with O'Neill's army
and presented an almost unconquerable front to the English
they foolishly landed in the hostile territory at the farthest
point they could from O'Neill, namely Kinsale. Mountjoy
was delighted and it is reported that he actually danced.
Gloom and depression now spread over O'Neill and his
followers. His one ray of hope, that the Spaniards would
sally out into the countryside, rally the southern Irish
chieftains, and give battle to Mountjoy, faded as day by day
passed and the Spaniards fortified themselves in Kinsale,
built walls, settled down for a long siege and sent word to
O'Neill to come and help them. What was O'Neill to do?
Was he to stay put and let the Spaniards fend for themselves? This would have incurred the wrath of Philip of
Spain and might turn his friendship into enmity. Was he to
undertake the terrible three hundred mile march in the
depth of winter to Kinsale, his men weary, exhausted,
famished and unfit for battle? He decided to try a feint and
he marched on the Pale, that part of Leinster around Dublin,
Louth and Meath which was colonised and inhabited by the
English, sacked towns and villages, plundered the livestock,
burned the corn and terrorised the inhabitants. He hoped
by this manoeuvre to draw off Mountjoy's army from

Kinsale, but Mountjoy did not react. However much personal sympathy he felt for his fellow countrymen in the Pale he knew that Kinsale was his place and that O'Neill would eventually have to come there. In this he was right. He consolidated his positions around Kinsale, fortified and dug in his men, and waited to see what O'Neill would do. His anxiety was soon to be relieved. O'Neill decided to march on Kinsale with all possible speed, despite the terrible winter of incessant rain which turned every river into a swollen torrent and turned the few roads that there were into slushy, mucky tracks. It is a mark of his sense of foreboding that before he left he made his will. But wily as ever, he split his forces in two and sent O'Donnell at the head of one half before him. Mountjoy got wind of this and at once dispatched a force under Carew to intercept him. Carew waited at Holycross on the River Suir where the river was fordable, and where O'Donnell was certain to pass because he could not cross the mountain — it being a mass of sodden, quaking earth from the rains. There on the evening of 21 November Carew waited for what was to him certain victory. But luck favoured O'Donnell for with nightfall came a terrible frost which hardened the ground and he swerved to the west and marched all night on the frozen terrain. When Carew realised he had been tricked he gave chase to O'Donnell but nowhere could he find him. O'Donnell had not rested. He kept marching non-stop the following day and night. Carew gave up all hope of catching him and manfully acknowledged O'Donnell's march as 'the greatest march that had ever been heard of'. Now O'Donnell was a good tactician but a poor strategist and had he been a military leader of high calibre he would have immediately swerved to the east and cut off Carew's retreat to Kinsale and trapped the English army between himself and O'Neill's oncoming forces. Between them they could have obliterated Carew's army, leaving Mountjoy with his skeleton forces at Kinsale, an easy prey. But instead he marched gaily due south towards Castlehaven, and Carew delightedly turned back to Kinsale. Mountjoy now began to have second thoughts about his position. He calculated that O'Neill and O'Donnell, moving rapidly on Kinsale, would soon surround him and cut off all his lines of supply and while he was pondering this situation the reality came upon him. O'Neill and O'Donnell joined forces at Innishannon and threw a net of troops around the English army. Mountjoy was trapped. The Spaniards were well housed inside the town with enough supplies to last two months. Mountjoy and his army were in the middle with only a few weeks victuals. Outside him were the Irish with access to unlimited supplies. O'Neill may well have smiled — all he had to do was wait until Mountjoy's army starved or surrendered. But at that moment the traditional curse of Ireland struck, the curse of dissention and disunity. O'Donnell, acting under the influence of the Spaniards, insisted on attacking and all the old Irish tribal pride and passion flared up. Tempers flashed, harsh words were spoken, O'Donnell with his fiery and passionate appeals swayed the majority of commanders and in the end O'Neill gave way. The disunity of the conference had its aftermath. O'Neill's heart was not in the fight. Briefly the plan was that the Irish and the Spaniards should attack simultaneously by night, but it was a scrappy plan, hastily conceived, and all the while at the conference there sat Brian Mac Hugh Oge Mahon, one of the Irish commanders silently listening to what passed, noting carefully the Irish plan. Like so many of his countrymen before him this traitor sold the plans to Mountjoy for the promise of a title and lands, so that, when the Irish did half-heartedly attack, the English army were in readiness and the result was a rout. Through a stupid misunderstanding the Spaniards failed to keep their part of the bargain and instead of simultaneously attacking they stayed quietly within their walls. The Irish losses were given as one thousand and the English as six men. Now the great question is why did O'Neill not pull himself together, regroup his forces and continue the siege? To this there is no satisfactory answer and we can only conjecture that he may have thought Fate was against him; not alone was he fighting the English, but he was also fighting O'Donnell, the Spaniards, the weather, everything. He collected the remnants of his army and marched home, defeated and disillusioned. Everything he had fought and lived for was lost. It is in a situation like this that one can fully grasp the truth of Napoleon's great dictum — 'In war the morale is to the physical as three is to one.' O'Donnell fled to Spain to get more help and Mountjoy at once sent his professional poisoner, Blake, after him, who in a few months caught up with O'Donnell and administered the deadly dose. The Spanish commander made friends with Mountjoy who let him return to Spain with his troops, arms and supplies. All O'Neill's lands and castles were confiscated and he fled to Rome where he died years later, a lonely, broken old man. Thus the Battle of Kinsale. Thus was established here the power of England. Three hundred years were to pass before another Irishman of O'Neill's calibre arose to eventually shake off the English yoke. Strangely enough this man, of whom I will speak again, was born but a very short distance from the scene of the Kinsale disaster. His birth-place was near the little village of Rosscarbery in a wild, picturesque, isolated part of West Cork.

2

On the evening of the fourth day there was a good weather forecast. The wind would go into the North-East force three to four, which of course would be ideal, as it would be blowing off the land so no big seas could build up, and by travelling with the ebb tide I would have smooth water all the way. One of the many things I have learned about cruising is to stay put in a harbour until the right wind and the right day comes along. This calls for a lot of patience but it is always worthwhile in the end. The miseries of the sea come to those who are in a hurry, as indeed do the miseries of many other sides of life.

Very shortly after dawn I was up and about. I stripped off, stood out in the cockpit, and poured three or four buckets of sea water over myself and, although I did this in full view of the street I felt sure that nobody in Kinsale would see anything that they were not well acquainted with already, if Mine Host of the pub were to be believed. After a good breakfast I stowed the punt on deck, readied the self-steering, set the main sail and hauled up the anchor. It was just eight o'clock. High water would be at nine and I would have six hours of strong ebb under me, and so I was off at last on the longest and hardest leg of my solo adventure.

When I reached the mouth of the harbour I put up the large foresail because the wind out here at sea was lighter than I expected it to be and I set my course for the Old Head of Kinsale which rose majestically out of the water, at the end of a long arm of land, some six or seven miles away. A strange kind of terror began to come over me again. Some writer once said that there is no such thing as fear, there is only a thing called time, which separates man from everything he craves. In this mood I thought of the lines of Dylan Thomas

Time held me green and dying
Though I sang in my chains like the sea

I find that in situations like this it sometimes helps me to reason with myself. *Dualla* was a first-class boat, solid, capable and sea-worthy, equipped with the best gear suitable to her size. I had taken every reasonable precaution that a man of the sea could take, I had a long experience of sailing and had weathered many storms in the past. I had prudently waited for the right day and the right wind and now I had it — everything was in my favour. With these encouraging thoughts in my mind I sat back and relaxed, and waited calmly for *Dualla*, now scudding along before a quartering wind, to reach the first moment of apprehension, namely the race off the Old Head of Kinsale, Let me explain. A tidal race is a mass of water tumbling and boiling in pyramidical confusion with no regularity whatever either in the set or the height of the waves. One wave comes charging at the boat from in front, another will hit it from the side, while yet another will crash over the stern sending cascasdes of water into the cockpit and cabin. A tidal race is least dangerous when the tide is turning, that short period of time known as 'slack water'. Neither is it too perilous when the wind is blowing from the same direction from which the tide is flowing; but it becomes positively treacherous and quite critical when the wind is blowing against the flow of the tide, and indeed large ocean-going ships have time and again been capsised and lost in tidal races. In a strong wind against a tide there is but one sensible course of action and that is to sail away many miles out to sea where the waves are once more setting with regularity. The race off the Old Head of Kinsale extends a distance of from two to four miles from the land and it was once my misfortune, many years ago, to get caught right in the middle of it. The wind was blowing a little over force five — it was an irregular drunken kind of wind, and there was a strong tide running in the opposite direction raising mountainous twisting seas. We had set a course to pass four miles off the Head and so sail clear of this menacing stretch of water. I was on the tiller, but, as so often happens at sea, I badly misjudged the distance and with appalling suddenness we found ourselves right in the mass of confused seas. We could not turn back without running the risk of being struck broadside on by a few tons of grey-green ocean and perhaps dispatched with maximum speed to the bottom. All we could do was to go right on. The tide was pulling the boat in one direction while the wind was pushing it in the opposite direction, the waves were high, confused and snarling at us like a pack of hungry wolves; we were tossed mercilessly up an down, back and forth in this seething mass of water. The ceaseless hammering and shaking, as wave after wave crashed on the deck, threw everything in the cabin into total disarray; most of the delph was smashed to pieces, our beds and bedclothes were flung helter-skelter around; our treasured bottles of liquor were broken to bits and their precious contents poured down into the bilges. For more than two hours we suffered this terrible beating edging our way forward inch by inch, until finally with equal suddenness we were out of it and back into smooth water once more. One experience like this was enough to give me a healthy respect for the seas off the Old Head of Kinsale, and as I now drew closer to it I was filled with apprehension. My worries were groundless. It was slack water, the wind was blowing off the land and the seas all around the Head perfectly calm and as I sailed around and into Courtmacsherry Bay I felt buoyant because I knew that unless conditions deteriorated rapidly, the other tidal races which I had to pass at the Seven Heads and the Galley Head would be equally calm.

I could now look forward to six hours of fair tide under me and a fair wind with me, and this should easily get me to Glandore. Courtmacsherry Bay looked beautiful in the morning sun. The curling smoke was beginning to arise from the cottages and farmsteads along the coastline announcing the start of a new day. The long white strands of Garrettstown, usually so crowded with people, were silent and deserted except for the sea birds in search of a morning meal. In the distance I could see Coolmain Castle dominating the landscape and I remembered that it was once the home of one of Ireland's most beloved writers, Donn Byrne, who met his death so tragically in this very bay. More than once I have made a literary pilgrimage to nearby Rathclarin church where he is buried. A simple Celtic cross, under the spreading leaves of a lime tree, marks his grave. Although he wrote in English he was a great lover of the Irish language and he chose as his epitaph the first line of his favourite song which is cut into the stone:

Tá mé i mo coladh agus ná dusigh mé

which translated means:

I am sleeping do not waken me

Here amid Irish lanes and hedgerows lulled by the sound of the sea and the singing of birds his epitaph is most nobly honoured and respected.

It is the end of us all. Our little lives are rounded, not by sleep, but by the terrifying reality of death which calls every child of Eve at the close of this restless life. Here I was, sitting at the helm on the most beautiful of summer days. The golden sand on the shoreline was edged with small silver waves. White clouds romped happily across the blue sky. The gentle off-shore wind filled *Dualla's* sails. Here in the midst of this sheer loveliness on land and sea my heart became heavy and my mind clouded. Memory began to take over and memory is the most powerful of all human faculties because it has the tremendous power to give back life to those who are dead.

Isn't it a strange thing how scenes of great beauty can quicken the heart to sorrow. Padraig Pearse must have felt this many times and he gave expression to it the night before he was executed in his touching poem *The Wayfarer*:

> *The beauty of this world hath made me sad,*
> *This beauty that will pass;*
> *Sometimes my heart hath shaken with great joy*
> *To see a leaping squirrel in a tree,*
> *Or a red lady-bird upon a stalk,*
> *Or little rabbits in a field at evening,*
> *Lit by a slanting sun,*
> *Or some green hill where shadows drifted by,*
> *Some quiet hill where mountainy man hath sown*
> *And soon will reap, near to the gate of Heaven;*
> *Or children with bare feet upon the sands*
> *Of some ebbed sea, or playing on the streets*
> *Of little towns in Connacht,*
> *Things young and happy.*

And then my heart hath told me:
These will pass,
Will pass and change,
Will die and be no more,
Things bright and green, things young and happy;
And I have gone upon my way
Sorrowful.

It may be indeed that the deep sadness experienced in the presence of great beauty is because we have no one to share it with. I have never known beauty to sadden two people in love. It is loneliness that saddens, and indeed causes a great deal of life's unhappiness, but loneliness is not something that we choose. It is normally forced upon us, and even on the most beautiful day it can fill the horizon with imaginary black clouds of sorrow.

Come mete out my loneliness, Oh wind,
For I would know
How far the living who must stay behind
Are from the dead who go.

The great danger of loneliness is not the sadness it induces, but the self-pity it generates. The lonely must face the reality of their pain and learn to live with it. 'True peace of mind comes from expecting the worst,' says Lin Yutang and Montaigne adds: 'My life has been full of terrible misfortunes, most of which never happened.' Every day has to be a new life to the lonely. There is no miraculous all-healing moment in the future. The miraculous moment is now.

There is this much, however, to say about a beautiful summers day. It can banish gloom and sadness as fast as it can bring it on. The whole magnificence of the rhythmic swaying sea, the myriad-shaped patchwork of the rolling West Cork countryside suddenly began to flood into my being while all the time the soft tender coastal wind ruffled the hair and caressed the skin. It is a wonderful experience to sail alone lost in dreams. You sail into a world of light on a blue sea and you dream the wildest dreams. You are a great lover with the world's most beautiful women at your feet; you are a superb athlete winning an Olympic race to the cheers of thousands of spectators; you are an explorer unveiling the innermost mysterious secrets of darkest Africa; you are a writer bringing joy and happiness to thousands; or a great statesman bringing peace and prosperity to your country. There is no limit to what you can be and there is no limit to what you can do. Have we all not dreamt such dreams at one time or another? Dreams can lift us to the clouds and beyond; but the reality quickly convinces us that we have feet of clay.

The hours slipped by under the captivating spell of this beautiful summer's day and I did not feel the time passing till I was rounding the Seven Heads where the sea was calm and there was no tidal race. Clonakilty Bay lay inside me but I kept well out in order to get full advantage of the strong tide under me. Just beyond the Heads I passed one of those commercial Sea Angling boats filled with well-fed pot-bellied tourists fishing for shark. This Sea Angling has become a great Government-backed attraction in Ireland inducing foreigners to come here and spend their money in brutal acts of savagery and slaughter. Surely we can find some other means of bringing visitors to Ireland than steeping them in blood? There must be some monstrous evil hidden down in the deepest depths of man that makes him the only creature in the universe who kills for sheer pleasure. The sharks themselves kill to eat and to survive, but man who is made in the image and likeness of God kills for pure kicks. These butchers, when their dirty slaughter is over, bring the dead sharks ashore, weigh them, and throw their wonderful blue majestic bodies into a rubbish heap to rot and then proceed to discuss with glee their savagery over a sumptuous dinner. Even the lion, who is the most ferocious animal of all, will pass you quietly by if he is not hungry and you do not threaten him. If God made man in his image and likeness then man has returned the compliment with a vengeance. Man may be the highest animal in the universe but he must surely be the lowest form of intellect.

There is no safe anchorage for yachts in Clonakilty Bay,

the only harbour being Ring and it is unsafe for two reasons. Firstly there is a bar across the entrance and the sea over it breaks in rough weather; a yacht caught on such a breaking sea would sink at once. Secondly, most of the harbour inside dries out, and this is a great pity for Ring is one of the most delightful old-world corners in all West Cork. Indeed this little hamlet holds an honoured place in Irish history for it was here in July 1920 that the West Cork I.R.A. made their first successful attack on a Coastguard station. The I.R.A. were badly armed and equipped and their attacks on Coastguard stations were made with the intention of capturing much-needed arms and ammunition. The I.R.A. moved at midnight, surrounded the station, while two brave men, Jim Murphy and 'Flyer' Nylan, rushed the door, burst it down, surprised the occupants and cleared the way for the rest of the section to get in and occupy the station. With all possible speed the raiding party searched and found a quantity of rifles and thousands of rounds of ammunition, and then made a fast get-away before the English troops, who were stationed only two miles away in Clonakilty, could get there. This was not a very spectacular action but it was the first of a series of attacks on Coast-guard stations and R.I.C. barracks which was to give vital equipment to the I.R.A. and to enable them to fight and win much more important battles such as those at Kilmichael and Crossbarry.

Just across from Ring is Inchydoney island and Clonakilty Harbour. Harbour is a bit of a misnomer since it is merely a vast expanse of mud flats, teaming with some of the most wonderful bird-life in the south. 'It affords more pleasure than profit,' wrote Smith in his *History of Cork.* 'The mouth of the river, being choked with sand, prevents vessels coming up to the town.' Sadly Inchydoney is now another loud, noisy tourist resort, with new bungalows, chalets, summer houses, camp and caravan sites and that curse of every Irish seaside place, the transistor.

On the west shore of Clonakilty Bay there is one delight-ful anchorage which is quite safe in winds between South-

West and North-West. It is an enchanting little inlet called Dunnycove Bay, and I remember once, many years ago, being unable to get around the Galley Head in a strong South-Westerly blow, which was getting worse and worse, and beginning to frighten the lives out of the three of us on board. As we approached the Head we could see through the field glasses, that the waves off the point were high, vicious and dangerous, so, like sensible men, we ran *Dualla* down the coast and anchored quite close to a little pier in Dunnycove in calm sheltered water. The wind blew stronger turning the whole bay into a mass of white foam and it was wonderful to sit on deck, with mugs of steaming hot tea and fresh lobster sandwiches, in the smoothest of water and look out at a raging sea only a few hundred yards away. As the storm showed no sign of easing we decided to stay overnight, and after supper rowed ashore and strolled along the little winding roads to a village where we accidentally met a friend who was on holidays in the area. He very kindly invited us to go with him in his car to a pub in Clonakilty where there was a ballad session in progress. For the yachtsman in a strange county, the pub is not an escape but a new and wonderous experience; new faces, new stories, new songs always await him in strange surroundings. In a crowded ale-house the beer was flowing freely and the singing voices of the drinkers gave the place an atmosphere of homeliness and companionship. This was not a phoney organised ballad session like you find in some modern tourist pubs designed to remove as much money as possible as quickly as possible from the pocket. It was healthy and spontaneous, and the singing came from the people themselves expressing their joys and sorrows, their past regrets and future hopes. As each man finished a song he called on someone else to start one and the crowd joined in the chorus and sang lustily and freely. We had barely seated ourselves when a tall angular fellow, who looked like a tree that was struck by lightning, was prevailed upon to contribute. Turning his back upon the crowd he bent down on one knee, covered the side of his face with his cap and let out a wail that bespoke the sorrows of several generations. It was a lament for a man executed for the murder of his wife:

> *You christian people one and all*
> *I hope you'll lend an ear*
> *To this my song and tragedy*
> *I mean to let you hear*
> *For the poisoning of his loving wife*
> *Richard Burke has suffered sore*
> *'Tis a caution is to man and wife*
> *Now and forever more.*
> *He gave the post-boy money*
> *To buy the strychnine*
> *He said it was for killing*
> *Some various bad vermin*
> *He told him to keep the change*
> *And the poison he brought home*
> *The half of it did her derange*
> *And made her writhe and moan.*

However, it appears as if the wife's sister caught him in the act and despite an offer of house and land and marriage decided to spill the beans — a fair warning to husbands not to trust their in-laws! The song ended to a different air and a different rhythm — one of the great charms of non-commercial ballad singing:

Let my death be now a warning to every married pair
To be guided by the holy Church and attentive unto prayer
The devil tempted me 'tis true both morning night and day
And from his wicked temptations I never could get away.
Good people may you never share in my sad grief and woe
Once in my time I never thought I'd die a public show,
But holy counsel had I took in time this could not be
This cruel death I would not get upon the gallows tree.

The lament for the death of Richard Burke seemed to have set a pattern for it was followed up by several other laments —strangely enough quite a number for the murder of a spouse, a loved one; Thomas Hayes for the murder of his wife, Patrick Kilkelly for the murder of his sweetheart, Jane McCullen for the murder of her child, Patrick Power for the murder of his father. Ireland must have been a rare old spot for murder and singing in the latter half of the nineteenth century when these songs were composed. As the hour for closing arrived several of the company, obviously reacting to the mournful tone of what went before, called upon a small wrinkled man with a face like a withered apple to sing *The Little Ball of Yarn*. This seemed to be the grand finale, and if I judged rightly, it was the grand finale of every session where the little man was present. Amid cheers and acclamations they stood him up on a half-barrel of porter and with a squeeky voice, like a broken-down melodian he sang his song. If it were only for the contrast with the other songs it is worth giving in full:

> *In the merry month of June*
> *When the roses were in bloom*
> *And the little birds were singing their sweet charms*
> *Sure I spied a pretty Miss*
> *And I kindly asked her this*
> *'May I wind up your little ball of yarn?'*
>
> *'Yerra no, kind sir,' said she*
> *'You're a stranger unto me*
> *And perhaps you've got some dearly other charmer.'*
> *'Yerra no, my turtle dove*
> *You're the only one I love*
> *And won't meddle with your little ball of yarn.'*
>
> *Now I took her to a grove*
> *Beneath a shady green*
> *With no intention of doing any harm*
> *And to my great surprise*
> *When I looked into her eyes*
> *I was winding up her little ball of yarn.*
>
> *Now nine months have passed and gone*
> *Since I met this fair young one*
> *And now she's holding a baby in her arms*

I said, 'My pretty Miss
Sure I never dreamed of this
When I was winding up your little ball of yarn.'

Now come all ye young and old
Take a warning when you're told
Never rise too early in the morn
Be like the blackbird and the thrush
Keep one hand upon your bush
And the other on your little ball of yarn.

I had now reached the Galley Head with its tall light-house resplendent in the sun, perched at the extremity of rugged, statuesque cliffs. Normally there is a bad tidal race here, impassible for a small boat under certain conditions, but today everything was calm. About a mile inside me and to the south-west of the head lay the dangerous Dhulic Rock with the seas breaking over it. The tide sets directly on the Dhulic and may the good God help any yacht that gets too close to it on the wrong side of that tide. Nature has constructed this rock with teeth like that of an enormous saw which would in a matter of seconds rip the bottom out of the strongest craft. It is however not a very serious danger to the yachtsman exercising a little care, for it shows above the surface at all stages of the tide and the breaking foam is visible a long distance out to sea and at night it can be avoided by keeping clear of the red section of the Galley lighthouse. It is however a hazard that brings a sigh of relief to a mariner only when he has passed it.

In the early nineteenth century when the lighthouse on the Galley Head was being built there was a sultan on holi-days with Lord Carbery in nearby Castlefreke Castle. He suggested that the beam of light should not only flash out to sea but also light up the countryside around, particular-ly Castlefreke itself. In those days the lords had almost absolute power and so the sultan's suggestion was put into immediate effect, and for generations the Galley beam not only consoled those at sea but also those living on the land.

When the lighthouse was being converted to electricity the planners decided to discontinue the land beam but there were so many protests from the occupants of lonely farms and homesteads, to whom the beam was such a vital source of comfort on a winter's night, that the planners reversed their decision and to this day the comforting beam shines on land and sea, probably the only lighthouse in the world to do so.

Castlefreke is now a roofless, windowless, crumbling ruin. I do not remember it in its heyday when it was the terror and tyranny of the countryside, when a casual decision taken at the brandy-and-coffee stage after dinner could affect the lives of hundreds of people, throw them out of their little homes and send them on the coffin ships to America or worse still on the slave ships to the West Indies. I came to it long after those days, during the second world war when I was in charge of training the Local Defence Force at their annual summer camps. The Castle was then owned by the Irish Government and the only piece of original furniture left was an unusually large portrait of an earlier Lord Carbery embedded in the masonry overlooking the main hallway. This portrait was riddled with bullet holes made by the lord himself. The story goes that when he got drunk, he suffered from depression and had a strong urge to commit suicide, but instead of shooting himself, he shot his portrait, thus enabling himself to get drunk and commit suicide as often as he pleased. In the end he died peacefully in bed, quite sober.

Each summer during the war Castlefreke was turned into a military encampment for the training of the Local Defence Force of West Cork. The period of training was short and intensive — one week only. Approximately three hundred Volunteers gathered there each Saturday and remained until the following Saturday during which time they trained in all forms of guerilla tactics, field-craft, endurance, night marching and every aspect of a soldier's training that would turn them into a first class resistance force should the country ever be invaded. Work began at 7 a.m. and concluded at 7 p.m. It was a twelve hour day and these young men got virtually nothing, except their board and keep, for giving up their annual holidays to serve their country. I spent the summer of 1943 in Castlefreke training them. It was a tense period when invasion might come at any moment and more than once we spotted the ominous periscopes of German submarines in numbers off the Galley Head, Churchill, like a barnyard turkey-cock, was beginning to display his arrogance in the first flush of a few minor victories, and the thought of invading us was constantly in his mind. Roosevelt was using every debasing means in his power to discredit De Valera and his policy of neutrality in the minds of the Irish Americans so as to prepare them for a probable invasion by the Allies. Everyone, not only in Castlefreke but throughout the entire army, was aware of this tense, dangerous and explosive situation. When I look back on those heroic days I know I should recall the loyalty, courage, devotion and sacrifice of the Irish soldiers who were all around me and whose life I shared; but by some strange quirk of human nature the thing I remember most was an incident which must surely mark the high water of governmental stupidity.

We had been warned verbally for quite some time that we were to expect an important government directive which was to be brought immediately to the notice of all ranks. No doubt, we thought, this was something of major concern, dealing with the repelling of an invasion which might have been imminent. At last the masterpiece arrived when the whole world was rocked asunder and thousands were slaughtered daily in the greatest carnage of history. As far as I can recall, here is the directive in full:

NEW INSTRUCTIONS
ON THE CLEANING OF WINDOWS
BY MILITARY PERSONNEL

1. The cleaning of the outside of windows of buildings will only be undertaken by two soldiers under the supervision and control of a Corporal or Sergeant.

2. The soldier cleaning the window will sit on the window-sill with his legs and feet inside the room.

3. Before going out on the sill a rope will be tied around the soldier's body and under his armpits. When the soldier is sitting on the sill the rope will be secured and the second soldier will firmly hold the rope as an additional precaution. Only sufficient play will be permitted in the rope so as to enable the soldier cleaning the window to carry out his work from the sitting position.

4. The cleaner will maintain a firm hold on the window with one hand and clean the window panes with the other hand.

5. When it is necessary to have the windows lowered or raised in order to have the cleaning carried out this operation will be performed by the Corporal or Sergeant in charge from the inside of the room.

6. When it is not possible to clean the upper part of a window, it will be cleaned from the inside by leaning outwards while standing on the inside. In this case the rope will be used in the same manner as outlined in (3) above.

7. Buckets, basins etc. will not be brought on to the outer sills with the cleaner. All cleaning material will be handed to the cleaner as required, by the Corporal or Sergeant in charge.

8. A further Directive will be issued at a later date concerning the cleaning of the following types of windows: Steel Casement Sashes, Sky or Lavatory Lights, windows of motor-cars, lorries and aeroplanes.

9. Members of the Local Defence Force, or soldiers who have not completed a basic six months military training will not be permitted to clean windows.

Many years later, I remarked to a high-ranking officer that I was determined to publish this Directive one day, somewhere. 'Be careful,' he replied with a broad grin on his face. 'Window-cleaning is a complex and confidential operation. You might be prosecuted under the Official Secrets Act.'

I was now sailing along past Rosscarbery Bay, past the

long delightful strands of Owenahincha which were beginning to come to life with the summer crowds. Papa, Mama and the toddlers were crowding the beaches and from the distance they looked like furtive ants scurrying around the edge of an ant hill. Then I heard an old familiar sound, a cry or wail of sadness and I knew I was close to Cloghna Rock, known in Irish as *Carrig Cliodhna*. This rock has been haunted for seven hundred years by the Irish goddess Cliodhna. The smart yachtsmen in their reefer jackets, flannel pants, red necktie and black shoes will tell you that the melancholy cry is caused by the tides rushing into the deep caves along the shore. Do not believe a word of this. A lone yachtsman like myself, went in one morning at dawn to investigate, and there he found Cliodhna, the most beautiful looking woman in the world, sitting on a rock in front of a cave crying her eyes out. She told him that she was keening the fate of an unfree Ireland and was destined to continue her mourning until the day when all Ireland is one. There's not a word of a lie in this for he told me every detail of what happpened himself. He consoled her as best he could and by God but it wasn't long till the two of them were madly in love with each other. He abandoned his yacht and went into the cave with Cliodhna and he was never seen again. There in the bowels of the earth in a place like *Tír-na-nÓg* they lived happily ever afterwards, Cliodhna coming out the odd time to fulfil her destiny by crying. The insurance people were delighted because there was no one to claim compensation for the yacht, and all the premiums were paid. You might ask me how I know all that if he were never seen again, but that's another story and another day's work.

When I sail through this historic bay I am always tempted to run up the long narrow creek and tie up at Rosscarbery pier. Unfortunately the pier dries out and with *Dualla* drawing five-and-a-half feet such indulgence would be foolhardy. In the past, however, and in a smaller boat I have tied up many times and I can earnestly recommend it to anyone who does not mind drying out alongside and who has plenty of time to explore the quaint village and surrounding countryside. Rosscarbery is steeped in history. It was the seat of a famous monastery and school as early as the sixth century when Cork was an unknown and unimportant hamlet. All around Rosscarbery are memories of our past; stone circles, churches, castles, strongholds, ring enclosures but for me the greatest relic of all is a more modern one — the ruined farmstead at Sams Cross where the saviour of modern Ireland, who reversed the defeat at Kinsale, Michael Collins, was born on 16 October 1890.

Every few hundred years or so in the course of our history destiny throws up a man of top-calibre; Niall of the Nine Hostages, Brian Boru, Owen Roe O'Neill, and in our century Michael Collins. It is not true to say that he alone won the war against the British but it is true to say that, were there no Michael Collins the Anglo-Irish War of 1916-1922 would have been just one more of these countless abortive attempts at freedom that ended in disaster and defeat during the previous centuries. Since Ireland was first invaded seven hundred years before, almost every generation broke out in revolution against the tyranny and cruelty of the oppressors, only to be beaten and clubbed into insensibility almost before they began. The central recurring reason for this failure was one which Collins, and only Collins, fully grasped. He had a tremendous sense of history and his detailed studies on the earlier revolutions brought out clearly one constant fact. *The Irish were defeated each time because their armies were riddled with British spies.* This was a truth, amazing in its simplicity, but a truth which never seems to have been grasped by the earlier revolutionary leaders. Collins saw it, grasped it, and dealt with it mercilessly and ruthlessly. To this task he bent his tremendous energy and organising ability and before they knew what was upon them every important British Military unit in Ireland was infiltrated by Collins' spies. All this had the effect that when units of the British army moved against the I.R.A. their movements were known in advance, and the trench-coated guerillas were waiting for them in carefully planned ambush sites. The British were now like blind men fighting those with full sight. For the first time in our history this great imperial army was defeated in battle after battle by the ill-clad, ill-equipped, but forewarned Irish guerillas. Britain poured more money, more men, more equipment into the war, but it was all to no avail. One by one British counter-intelligence agents in Ireland were shot on Collin's orders, so that by the summer of 1920 the British army in Ireland was demoralised and defeated, the British intelligence service crippled and their best agents dead. Churchill estimated at the time that it would take 250,000 men to hold Ireland and that this force would have to be replaced every year. The cabinet in London decided that it was no longer worth it, but before giving up they gambled one last fling. They knew if they could get Collins, victory would be theirs within a year. They raised the reward on his head to £10,000, the equivalent of £150,000 of our money today, and assembled in Cairo, Egypt, sixteen of their top intelligence officers. This group was told from the start that their destination was Ireland, and their objective the capture, dead or alive, of Collins. They underwent a six-week intensive course of study on Michael Collins, his appearance, his habits, his friends, his methods and when they completed this course they set out for Ireland. They travelled *incognito* as civilians under false names, and arrived in Dublin on different dates. Some of them booked in at hotels, others in rented flats. But Collins was one step ahead of them. His own spies provided him with the names and addresses of all sixteen. Then, on Sunday, 21 November 1920 eight squads of the Dublin I.R.A. Brigade struck and shot fourteen of the sixteen British spies in their bedrooms. The end of the British intelligence service in Ireland had come. The spell of hundreds of years was at last broken. Collin's own words on the incident are revealing:

'By their destruction the very air is made sweeter. That should be the future's judgement on this particular event.

For myself my conscience is clear. There is no crime in detecting and destroying the spy and the informer. They have destroyed without trial. I have paid them back in their own coin.'

The following year, Lloyd George, the treacherous British prime minister, opened negotiations with the Irish leaders for peace. From these protracted negotiations came a truce, and after the truce the signing of the Treaty by Collins and his associates. There is something of the Greek tragedy in his prophetic remark after he had signed the document: 'I have signed my death warrant.' For indeed he had. He was a committed Republican who regarded the Treaty, not as a final settlement, but as a means to an end. He was opposed by his former comrades-in-arms and the bitter Civil War ensued. His heart was not in this senseless struggle. From the beginning he kept contact, through intermediaries, with the leaders of the Anti-Treaty forces, always hoping that he could bring about a peaceful and honourable settlement. On 22 August 1922, he was in his own West Cork, and had a secret appointment that evening with a number of top Anti-Treaty officers in Desmond's Hotel, Cork. Had this meeting taken place it is more than likely that the Civil War would have ended, but on his way to the meeting he was ambushed at Beal-na-mBláth, and on that beautiful autumn evening, he died from a bullet which tore a huge gash in his head and neck. His opponent De Valera, was hiding in North Cork at the time and the following day when an aide, in a jubilant mood, brought him the news, Dev burst into tears and said: 'It's a sad day for us when any Irishman would rejoice at the death of Michael Collins.'

Dualla was now sailing happily along the beautiful West Cork coast in a stiffening breeze and glorious sunshine and I was feeling a little sad that her draft would not allow me to linger on and visit the beautiful inlets of Castle Bay, Mill Cove and Tralong Bay which seemed to beckon invitingly at me. I always feel a sense of loss at having to leave unexplored such charming little creeks and somewhere in the dark depths of my unconscious mind there lurks a feeling of guilt at my failure to follow my heart. We all complain that in our daily lives we are forced to keep pushing on, and yet, here, in our leisure hours we commit the self-same offence and leave behind us:

> *Charmed magic casements, opening on the foam*
> *Of perilous seas, in fairy lands forlorn.*

I set my course for Adam Island at the entrance to Glandore Harbour, an island surrounded by submerged rocks and dangerous reefs. Further in there is Eve Island which is clear all round and the local advice to mariners is: 'Avoid Adam — Hug Eve.' I followed this advice and soon dropped anchor off Glandore pier in the most beautiful woodland setting one could imagine. I had now completed the longest and most dangerous part of my solo cruise. If I felt like Chichester in Kinsale I felt like Columbus in Glandore.

3

I stayed two days in Glandore which is one of the most delightful harbours in West Cork. The best anchorage is in a bight south-west of the pier where the friendly woods reach down to the sea like long arms stretched out in welcome. Glandore, lacking sandy beaches, has not yet become a dumping ground for tourists and transistors, and is still a haven for those who seek a little peace. I think it was Daniel Corkery who somewhere described it as 'one of Ireland's secret places, without traffic, almost without the pulse of life'. There are some corners of the Irish coast that one can actually love with a physical love and Glandore is one of them. The scent of the wild woodbine mixed with that of roses and lilac is enough to make an old man feel young and to remember evenings of long ago when the wild throbbing joy of first love brought a happiness that would never be known again. Glandore is the kind of place that makes you want to say: 'Here I wish to live and love and die'. It is the kind of place that fills the soul with ecstasy, the kind of place when you sail away from it you have the feeling that you have just missed total happiness by mere seconds.

The countryside around Glandore is dotted with anti-quities, but antiquities in themselves do not attract me. They are mostly the gaunt symbols of pain and sorrow, famine and pestilence, slaughter and death and they only serve to remind me that we haven't learned one single lesson from the tragedies that men enacted all around them. When the defiant Archbishop Croke of Cashel was having an altercation with Leo XIII, the Pope in an attempt to pacify him offered him relics of St Peter and St Paul as a parting gift. 'Keep them,' replied Croke. 'We have more martyrs' bones in one square mile of Irish ground than you have in the whole of Rome.' But for me Glandore is not the place of martyrs' bones or of 'old unhappy far-off things' but the home of two unique men who spent their lives and fortunes in trying to ease the misery and sufferings of the Irish peasant. One was the God-fearing, church-going Christ-ian, James Redmond Barry, the other, the bizarre, outland-ish, agnostic William Thompson.

James Barry was born near the Seven Heads in 1789. He inherited large estates and great wealth which he could have dissipated as his fellow landlords did in drinking, gambling and whoring. Instead he dedicated himself to the task of trying at least to make life bearable for the hoards of famished starving people that eked out an existence little better than the animals. He began by reviving the fishing industry in Glandore, and had a new pier and slipway built and further up at Union Hall he started a boatyard to build

47

half-decked boats which were leased out to the fisherman. He arranged for the marketing of their catches so that no middleman could come along and skim off the cream, and within a few years virtually every able-bodied fisherman was at work and earning an adequate living and it is to their eternal credit that hardly any of them failed in his repayments. Barry then turned his attention to the farming community, who were living in filthy hovels and who kept them filthy for fear the exorbitant rent they were already paying would be further increased. He divided up his estates into economic units of model farms, and built small but adequate houses on each farm. He stocked the farms by giving the occupiers interest free loans and it is recorded that out of seventy such farms only one or two failed in their repayments and in each case the failure was due to a family death. He designed, laid out and rebuilt Glandore village, planted the woodlands and built a National School which was still in use up to fifteen years ago. But his great dream was destroyed by the famine, and nothing he could do could save the lives of the people who died in their thousands in one of the greatest acts of political genocide in the history of the human race. He lived to the great age of ninety only to see his beloved Glandore, his boatyards, his fishing industry in ruins. It is rather sad that nowhere in Glandore is there any plaque, memorial or memento to this great landlord. *Sic transit gloria mundi.*

William Thompson was a different kettle of fish. He was born in Cork in 1775 and when he was in his late thirties he inherited an estate of 15,000 acres around Glandore. Thompson could be accurately described as the first modern communist. His well-written and scholarly book, *Principles of the Distribution of Wealth* said in effect what Marx said half a century later. Indeed the Webbs described Marx as 'a distinguished disciple of William Thompson'. When he inherited these vast estates he determined to become, not another absentee landlord, but to stay at home and put the principles of communism into practice among his tenants. He experimented with collective farms, com-

48

munal ownership, equal distribution of monies and all the other paraphernalia of the theory of communism. This great experiment failed largely because he lacked any practical strain but also because he was an outlandish eccentric. He dressed sometimes with his clothes back to front, he carried the Tricolour on his walking stick, refused to eat meat, eggs or butter and performed various chemical experiments in public so that the simple folk thought he was either a vampire or a male witch. His communal holdings ran foul of the church when he advised the West Cork farmers to share wives and practise birth control. His description of priests as 'rapacious parasites and dealers in brimstone' did nothing to endear him to the See of Peter. Strangely enough he supported O'Connell in his fight for Catholic Emancipation which was probably the reason he was given a church funeral when he died. A few days later when his will was read there was consternation. In it he forbade any priest or parson to pray over or interfere with his remains and in haste the church authorities removed his body from consecrated ground. His will also provided for his skeleton to be preserved and covered with silver ornaments so that it might present a fashionable appearance and be sent to a lady friend in England as a keepsake. It was in fact delivered to her by special courier and until her death held an honoured place in her bedroom. He left his estates and fortune to his communal movement but this part of the will was contested by his relatives and the litigation dragged on so long that, like many another fortune, the lawyers collected the lot. Glandore has not as yet erected a monument to him, but if you happen to be in Prague call in to the International Communist Museum and there you will find, in a place of distinction, a magnificent bust of William Thompson, the first Irish communist.

I took a stroll up north of the village where in a beautiful setting amid clusters of rhododendrons I had a look at Shorecliffe House where in 1919 the famous West Cork Brigade of the I.R.A. held their first training camp. This was a bold and daring move because most of them were wanted men with a price on their heads. Dick McKee, who was later tortured and executed, was in charge of the camp and devised a programme of training consisting in the main of guerilla tactics, endurance tests, and mine warfare. They were about to congratulate themselves on having success-fully concealed their activities from the enemy when one morning they woke up to find themselves surrounded by a ring of steel; the British army together with the R.I.C. had thrown a cordon around the whole camp and sealed off every possible exit. The I.R.A. had taken the precaution of having no arms with them and pretended they were there to attend an Irish language course. Since they were all strangers to the area the local British intelligence man, Sergeant Mul-hern, could only identify a few of them, who were arrested and later sent to prison. But there was no evidence as to who the rest were or what they were doing there; neverthe-less the British soldiers rough-handled and beat them up as well as destroying all their cooking equipment. In the midst of this search there was a strange movement seen in a rhododendron bush. The British surrounded it immediately with machine-gunners possibly believing that they had at last found the evidence they required. On one side of the bush two hob-nailed boots stuck out and a number of soldiers rushed forward and dragged out a bleary-eyed little man who proved to be none other than the famous Irish novelist and short story writer Seán-Padraic Ó Conaire sleeping off last night's drunk. Padraic was a bohemian who rambled around the country and slept in haybarns and ditches as the mood took him. Evidently he found a nice comfortable spot to sleep the night before not knowing he was in the middle of an I.R.A. camp. The humour of the situation started loud guffaws of laughter and the British army withdrew leaving the campers to clean up the mess and finish their training. The presence of Padraic lent evidence to the story that the men were only learning Irish.

On my second day in Glandore I moved *Dualla* to the head of the inlet and anchored her just off the little stone pier at Union Hall, which is the safest anchorage in the whole harbour for no matter what way the wind blows it is so sheltered that there is no chance of any strong sea getting up. Union Hall is a delightful little fishing hamlet as yet untouched by tourism. From the end of the pier you walk up a picturesque little byroad to reach the village itself which is snugly nestled into the surrounding hills. Union Hall once had its great hour of glory and missed by inches, one might say, becoming a world famous place of pilgrimage like Lourdes or Knock. In the year of 1832 a poor simple man named Thomas Harrington lived with his mother in a small two-roomed cabin at the foot of Ardagh Hill just outside the village. Harrington was dying a slow lingering death from consumption which was the merciless killer of those days, and he was, it seems, a man of high personal holiness who was constantly happy and serene despite his great sufferings and destitution. While he was dying the strangest lights of variable and ghastly colour were seen from time to time playing on the walls of his room and around his sick bed. News of this phenomenon spread far and wide in West Cork and literally thousands of sightseers came to visit the cabin. Some saw nothing, others only a faint pale light, while still others saw stars, meteors and balls of fire jumping about the room, and even though the most thorough investigations for fraud were carried out by priests, doctors, scientists and journalists nothing could be found that would explain the lights. Every inch of the cabin was searched, the walls, floor and roof were fine-combed without turning up a clue, and the mysterious lights remained until Harrington died but they were never seen afterwards. I was curious about these happenings and I wanted to find out more, I also wished to see the remains of the cabin and, if possible, Harrington's grave, so I betook myself into an inviting pub where I hoped I would strike up an acquaintance with some of the locals and maybe with a little luck and the loosening of tongues which is such a part of Irish pub life I might find out a little more. But unfortunately, or perhaps fortunately, I ran into the tail-end of a country wedding and in a very short time indeed I had forgotten Harrington and his lights.

The happy couple were both a little beyond the prime of life, I was told by a farmer with a navy blue suit, white shirt, speckled tie and a geranium in his button hole. 'They're passed the canonical age,' he said with a grin. They were gone to Cork for the day on their honeymoon and they'd get the last bus home in the evening because she'd have bonhams to feed and a lot of milking to do in the morning. The pub was crowded, the drink was flowing and it was clear that many an old friendship was being renewed and many an old enmity forgotten. The plump women folk, their hats decorated with ribbons and flowers looking like a bush over a holy well, sat together in one corner sipping ginger wine and gossiping. I sat down in another corner beside a little old man who was finishing a pint.

'Are you one of the wedding party?' I asked curiously.

'Well yes and no,' he replied. 'I'm not related or anything like that but 'twas I made the match.'

'Don't tell me you're a matchmaker?' I queried.

'Well I am, now, in me spare time,' he answered. 'But I was doing it all the time when I was young. You see I'm not from this county at all. They only called me in because they didn't want the neighbours to know what was up in case things went wrong, don't you see?'

He finished his pint and I called for another.

'Is it hard to make a match?' I asked, earnestly determined to draw him out to the full. He filled his pipe, reddened it, surveyed the pint and was off at a gallop.

'Yerra man alive,' he replied, 'you'd want the brains of De Valera and you'd want to be as cute as the Goban Saor was in judging asses. Some of the women do be as dry as the bones of a tinker, and more them does be as green as a garden of cabbage. Some of the ould bachelors couldn't afford to buy a candle or a box of matches for Christmas Night and more of them are so mean that they'd take the shirt off your arse and the skin off your nose. 'Tis no job for a fool is matchmaking.'

'It can't be that hard,' I said egging him on. 'Don't the people come to you themselves and sure all you have to do is make them shake hands.'

''Tis little you know, me dacent man,' he said now in full steam. 'Suppose there was an ould couple with two sons — well the eldest would get the farm and as soon as the ould couple got the pension they'd give a *gabhail* of money to the next fellow so that he could get a woman and marry into her farm. He'd come to me then and I'd have to find a woman with a dacent bit of land. More than likely she'd have her father and mother livin' with her. I'd ramble up to see them on a Sunday evening by way of no harm. We'd talk about the weather, and politics and the price of pigs and anything else that would come into our minds. Mind you they'd know bloody well what I was there for. The girl would be all shy and red in the face and after a while she'd gather herself up into the room out of the way and then I'd tell the ould couple I had word of a match. Himself would want to know who the fellow was and how much he had. I'd mention a figure well below what we had in mind so as to give myself a bit of room for bargaining. If he was agreeable he'd say he'd want a lot more but we could talk about that later. Then the next Sunday, when the mother and daughter would be gone to second Mass, I'd call up with me bould bachelor and himself and meself and the girl's father would walk the land. We'd have to do that to satisfy my man that he wasn't getting a pig in a poke, and that the land was well fenced and watered, with no ragworth, thistles or bouchalauns. We'd have a look at the outhouses and all the stock and if my man was satisfied then I'd arrange with the girl's father to come another day by myself to talk about the arrangements. Man alive 'tis then the trouble would start and I might have to make several journeys before we'd finally fix on the sum of money the bachelor would bring with him. Anyway when we had all that fixed we'd name a day to go to town to draw up the writings.'

'I don't rightly understand,' I queried.

'You see, we'd have to go to a solicitor to put everything in writin'. You could never trust the word of a mountainy farmer, for he's so crooked that if he said the Rosary with you he'd try to do you out of a decade. Anyway we'd all go to town, meself, the bachelor, the girl with her father and mother into a solicitor's office and everything would be put down on paper. The farm would be made over to the two when they married, the dowry would be lodged in the bank in the two names, the ould couple would have the right to be fed and to keep their pension and they'd also have the right to one room in the house and a seat in the car to Mass on Sunday, and a whole lot of other things like that. Then they'd all have to write their names on the piece of paper the solicitor would put in front of them and when that was over we'd go to an eatin' house for a feed of pig's head and cabbage and after that into the best pub in town for a bit of a celebration. We'd try to leave the couple alone so as they'd get to know one another. At first they'd be very shy and he'd be looking at her like a cat studyin' a saucer of boiled milk. After a while they'd soften out and he'd start to call her by her first name and then they'd be no stoppin' him. A week before the wedding the girl's parents would give a bit of a dance in the kitchen and all the neighbours would come for a night's devarsion. About midnight the strawboys would come – that is the local lads with their faces and chests covered with straw, and each one of them would dance with the bride-to-be and if she could make out who any of them was 'twould be a sign of bad luck. Some time during the night the neighbouring ould women would bring the girl into a back room and give her the goin'-on-strips.'

'What do you mean by goin'-on-strips?' I asked knowing damn well what he meant.

'Ah blast it,' he answered, 'they'd have to tell her what to do the first night. There's some women and they think 'tis through their navel they have children and indeed I may tell you that there's ould mountainy bachelors who think 'tis for stirring their tay God gave it to them.'

'And how much do you get out of all this,' I asked.

'Two shillings in the pound of the dowry money,' he replied. 'And two shillings in the pound of the value of the stock. Oh I'm not complainin'. I do alright, but 'tis bloody tough work. Of course I don't get paid 'til the day of the wedding. By the way I got paid this morning for this wedding. Will I stand you another drink?'

The pints were filled again. I knew there was a lot more to him, that he was unique of his kind and I was determined to press on.

'Tell me,' I said. 'Did you ever have any trouble after the wedding? What I mean is did all the marriages you made turn out alright?'

'The most of 'em did,' he replied. 'The most of 'em did. But a few times things went a bit contrary. I remember one time I made a match between a fairly crabbed farmer who lived alone and a nice young girl just turned forty. She would be moving in to his farm so she had to bring a dowry, and after a lot of argument her father — he was no great shapes; he never shook hands with a bank manager — agreed to give fourteen bullocks dowry, to be handed over the week of the marriage. Anyway about three months after the wedding didn't she come cycling into the yard to me one cold winter's morning and tell me that your man never touched her nor got into bed with her since they were married. She asked me to go down and have a chat with him for she was anxious to have a child before 'twas too late. Don't you understand she was gettin' on. Although 'twas no part of my work as a matchmaker still an' all I didn't mind giving a bit of after-sales service, as you might call it, so one day I was at a funeral in the neighbourhood and I called in to have a word with me boyo. He was in the haggard up to his knees in cowshit forking it into an ass and butt. I told him straight out that his missus came up to me with her little predicament and I asked him if it was true. "'Tis indeed," he answered calmly, "every word of it is true."

'"Damnit man," I said. "She's a woman, she wants a child and surely you want a son to leave the farm to when

55

you die."

'He looked staight at me and said: "You made the match, didn't you?"

'"I did indeed," I said.

'"Well you remember that her father promised to send me down fourteen bullocks as a dowry the week of the marriage?"

'"That's true," I said. "'Tis all in the writin's."

'"Well he only sent down twelve," answered me man. "An' until he sends down the other two bullocks damn the button will I open."

'I declare to me God I nearly burst out laughing in his face, but business is business and I went up to her father to see if I could get the two bullocks. Of course I couldn't tell him the truth of the matter don't you see, for he'd tell the whole countryside and make a laughing stock of his son-in-law, so I ups to him and I said that all the neighbours were saying that he was too poor, and that he couldn't afford to send down the two bullocks. That stung him, I tell you, and there and then he went into the paddock and turned out two fine strappin' bullocks to me. You should see the look of happiness on the woman's face when I drove the bullocks into the yard. Her eyes were dancin' in her head for she could be expecting a bit of fun from now on. Me bucko's face got ten years younger when he saw the two fine animals, and fair is fair, he sparked at once like a champion plug. Nine months later almost to the very day she had a young son, God bless him, and would you believe it, I was asked to stand for the child at the christening, and dacent enough, they sent me a present of a gander the next Christmas.'

Our pints were empty and we filled them again, now for the last time. The closing hour was upon us and the owner was trying to ease the more drunken members of the party on to the street.

'Do you know what I had to do these last few years?' my friend confided to me in a whisper. 'Any man over fifty that would come to me looking for a wife I'd ask him to strip off first before I'd make any move. You see I made a match between a cobbler and a respectable farmer's daughter a few years ago, who had £2,000 and brought it with her. A month after the wedding she came up to me in a fierce temper and demanded back the money she paid me for making the match, for she said that he spent the whole month on top of her grunting and snorting but couldn't do a damn thing. One night when he was in a drunken sleep she pulled back the bedclothes, took down the Sacred Heart lamp, and had a good look at him. Well according to her what he had was so small that she had to put on her glasses to see it. She left him there and then and I had to give her back the fee she paid me for she claimed I sold her defective goods. Ever since then I insist on inspecting things for myself to make sure the necessary implements are there, and in good order too.'

We had by now slowly made our way through the half-drunken crowd into the dimly lit street. A few of the men, propped up by their wives, were incoherently singing *The Boys of the County Cork*. Across the road the drunken farmer with the geranium in his buttonhole was relieving himself up against a telegraph pole and giving a tipsy rendering of *Faith of Our Fathers*.

'Tell me,' said the matchmaker, 'I suppose you're married yourself.'

'No,' I answered. 'I'm a widower.'

'Ah poor woman,' he said. 'So you buried her. God rest her soul. I'm sorry for your trouble.'

He edged me slowly into a darker corner of the street.

'You know,' he said. 'If ever you feel like sparkin' again I think I could fix you up. I have a widow with a fine snug farm and a house on me books, living by herself with no encumbrances. There are only two things I should tell you about her. She cast a shoe when she was young, that is she had a child you know, but sure that's no harm. The youngster was adopted by wealthy Yanks and is in America these years. The second thing is that she talks crooked, she has a very bad stutter. But I always say that that's an advantage

57

since she can't answer you back too quickly if you're having a row. There was a great story going round the parish the time she had the child. They said she was having a tally with a fellow in a haybarn and she got the child because on account of her stutter it took her too long to say: "S...s...stop! N...no...no!" Isn't that a good one for you now. Anyway she married a respectable farmer afterwards and he died, poor man, without giving her a family. She has a nice snug farm, well watered and sheltered, and plenty of money. If you're interested you know where to find me.'

'Would I have to strip off like the rest of them,' I asked.

'Ah, you divil you. I wouldn't ask you to do that,' he answered with a broad grin. 'I'd say you have the necessary machinery, and more. Anyway you know where to find me if you want me. Good night now and good luck.'

'Good night,' I said shaking his hand, 'and thanks for a lovely evening.'

I walked down the long dark byroad to the little stone pier. The night sky was studded with stars. Over my head a million worlds danced; worlds upon worlds upon worlds extending without end into the vast measureless infinitude of space. The only sound to break the silence was the patter of my sandalled feet barely audible through the long eerie shadows. As I rowed out to *Dualla* the oars skimming the surface of the water threw up bright flames of phosphorus which left long trails of dancing light on the still, calm sea. On board I sat out in the cockpit and absorbed the beauty of the night. The little harbour was like fairyland. A soft brilliant moon peeped out from a starry sky. The other boats outlined the shadows of their masts against the many openings on the richly wooded shore. The water was ablaze with phosphorus. The air was soft and affectionate. The magic and mystery of this bewitching scene reached down to the very depths of the soul and stirred up strange longings that defied the power of human understanding. And I remembered how, in the past, in this very harbour, she had shared such beauty with me. Now, she was gone and I was here. Once, on such a night as this, she spoke aloud the immortal words of Keats when he saw the first tell-tale spot of blood on his pillow and knew that death was upon him. I gazed up at the star-studded sky, and quite unconsciously found myself repeating those very words in my inner heart:

> When I behold, upon the night's starr'd face
> Huge cloudy symbols of a high romance
> And think that I may never live to trace
> Their shadows, with the magic hand of chance.
> And when I feel, fair Creature of an hour!
> That I shall never look upon thee more,
> Never have relish in the fairy power
> Of unreflecting love – then on the shore
> Of the wide world I stand alone and think
> Till Love and Fame to nothingness do sink.

4

The rays of a warm friendly sun, streaming across my bunk woke me early next morning, and without hurry, for that is the essence of cruising, I made a good Irish breakfast; rashers, eggs and strong coffee and sat out in the cockpit to share it with all nature. The birds of the sea, the gulls, the skuas, the terns, the kittiwakes, swooping and diving around me have to be fed too and by some strange primeval instinct they know that the yachtsman is their friend. The wind had changed and was blowing lightly from the South-West so having set the mainsail I prepared the largest foresail, brought up the anchor and glided smoothly out of the sheltered harbour over the morning waves into the open sea.

I skirted carefully around Sheela Point and Rabbit Island

in order to avoid the many concealed rocks which lie in wait for the unwary all along this beautiful but dangerous corner. I peeped into Carrigillihy Cove where now only two or three families live but where, in the last century, a thriving community of nearly a thousand souls made a good living from legitimate fishing and from that ever-green stand-by of the Irish coast dweller, illegitimate smuggling.

In those days of British occupation it was considered a patriotic duty to smuggle. Was this not depriving the hated regime of revenue? Indeed smuggling was a way of life along the whole south-west coast of Cork, with its many inlets open to vessels from France, Spain or Portugal and too far away or too inaccessible for the revenue men. On one occasion the king's servants got a tip off that a large consignment of brandy was about to be landed at Carrigillihy and Squince and they surrounded the area in force. The fishermen, seeing what was afoot, went out after dark and collected their brandy from the French ships at sea, but instead of landing it, they sank the casks and buoyed them up so that they could lift them when the danger was past. When they returned to harbour they were pounced on by the revenue men and police who only found each boat full of lobster pots for baiting. The customs men hastily made their way further west to Lough Hyne believing that the information they got was a plant to divert them. The following day a violent southerly gale blew up which broke the lashings on the casks and hurdled them ashore, and the good news spread like lightning so for the next two days and nights the entire population of Union Hall, Squince and Carrigillihy had the greatest orgy of drunkenness ever heard of in West Cork. Even the women and children it is said, were taking both sides of the road. A troop of soldiers had to come from Skibbereen to keep the peace and the final outcome was three dead, fifty-two in hospital and thirty-six in jail. But not a drop of brandy could be found anywhere.

There are so many lovely little harbours and inlets around here that I often wished I had a small motor-boat so that I could explore them fully. When I gaze longingly at this majestic coast line, its rugged cliffs, its seductive tempting caves I feel transported to another world, to the childhood world of *Treasure Island*. Their very mysteriousness seems to call me towards them to invite me to explore their hidden inscrutable secrets, to discover the buried treasure of a thousand years, the whitening bones of some dark and fiery pirate and perhaps, like the gallant knights of old, to rescue some beautiful maiden in distress. And then from the dark recesses of my memory came Goethe's touching poem of a lovely mermaid and a timid sailor:

> *Bathes not the golden sun his face —*
> *The moon too in the sea*
> *And rise they not from their resting place*
> *More beautiful to see?*
> *And lures you not the clear deep heaven*
> *Within the waters blue*
> *And your form so fair, so mirrored there*
> *In that eternal dew!*
> *The water rolled — the water swelled*
> *It reached his naked feet;*
> *He felt as at his loves approach*
> *His bounding bosom beat;*
> *She spoke to him, she sang to him,*
> *His short suspense is o'er;*
> *Half drew she him, half dropped he in,*
> *And sank to rise no more.*

There is no doubt about it most of us are incurable romantics. We love to contemplate the dream but few of us ever make it a reality. If I were a practical sensible man I would anchor *Dualla* close by and start my exploring in the rubber punt. Why do I not do it? Maybe because I realise, anyway, that the dream is unreal and only has an existence in the mind, or maybe because I fear there just might be an alluring maiden, hidden amongst the crags, who would call my bluff. There are hundreds of other exciting things I want to do and never succeed in doing any of them. Anything I've ever accomplished has only been after constant failure and disappointment, and I envy those who can set themselves a task and complete it with a minimum of difficulty. Somehow I've always had to try and try again. Nothing ever comes easily to me, and if I do realise some measure of success in some achievement it is usually the result of a happy accident.

Castlehaven is only an hour's run from Glandore in favourable winds but as it was blowing from the South-West I had to sail a long tack out to sea until I could lay Reen Point which marks the entrance to the harbour. Although the wind was against me the sailing was delightful and *Dualla* plunged her way through the ocean's breast, her wake glittering like a jet-stream in the sun. A fresh warm breeze blew across my face and the dancing sunbeams sparkled like silver droplets on the blue sea.

The great difference between sailing alone and sailing with companions is that when you are alone your thoughts turn in upon yourself. There is nobody to converse with and in searching your own soul you give yourself a kind of spiritual turkish bath, which, if it does not solve any problems, will at least refresh you. Sitting there in the cockpit, with one hand gently steering *Dualla* my mind went back fathom by fathom on the anchor rope of memory, and always in these moments of contemplation I think I see a light at the end of the long dark tunnel of uncertainty but more often than not in the past it turned out to be the light of a train rushing onwards to destroy all before it. If there is certainty it always seems to elude me. Where does one find Truth and how does one begin to search for it? How do we distinguish between real Truth and some kind of intellectual aspirin that looks like it? There is no immediate or definite answer to this terrifying question which poses itself time and again with unrelenting force to every living human being. Each has his own vision of life and what it should be for him, based upon his reading, his reflection and above all upon his experience of living. It would be presumptuous of him to try and foist off on others the road which he has found to be the right one for himself and for himself only. In the darkness, confusion and chaos of my own soul, when I found myself adrift from life and rebelling against everything, I accidentally came across an American book which was to influence me more than anything I had ever read and which was to point out a path that could help me to get out of the spirtual quicksands in which I was floundering. The book was *The Pursuit of Meaning* by Joseph Fabry and it helped me so much that I arranged to have it published separately here in Ireland so that many others might be able to share the inspiration it gave me. But first a little background. In the last century, Freud, the Viennese psychologist, put forward a theory which was to have a profound influence on the thinking world. Briefly he held that the motivating force in every human being's life was the pursuit of Pleasure, particularly sexual pleasure. Some time later he was followed by another renowned Viennese psychologist. Adler, who held that the motivating force in every human life was the pursuit of Power, and that all pleasure, sexual or otherwise, and indeed all man's activities, were but thinly disguised facets of his search for Power. Towards the middle of this present century yet another brilliant Viennese psychologist arose, Viktor Frankl, who disagreed with both these theories and who held that the motivating force in every human being's life was his search for Meaning, and that man's occupation with Pleasure and Power were in reality mere aspects of his search for Meaning. Joseph Fabry's book, *The Pursuit of Meaning*, is an explanation of Frankl's teachings. Frankl is an academic who wrote for academics and specialists, but Fabry explains it to the man in the street. The sheer excitement I experienced as I read this book was beyond words. I have read it again and again and each time I take it up I find something new and constructive. The book starts off by showing us that our feelings of emptiness, depression, despair and anger are nothing to be ashamed of. There is in fact a certain normality about such feelings and they are indeed a proof of our humanness, and a proof that we are searching for something worthwhile which we have not yet found. The way to come to terms with these feelings is not to run away from them through drink, drugs, sex, frivolous entertainment, wasteful feverish activities, or self-pity. This existential vacuum in our lives can only be filled with something satisfying and that magical something is the experience of finding a Meaning in life. Meaning is something that cannot be invented and each person must discover it for himself. How to discover it is one of the main themes of the book. It shows that in order to discover a Meaning in life we must discover our own selves first, honestly and truthfully, stop running away and stop throwing dust in our own eyes. This is the first step and for some of us it can be hard, as we seem to have an infinite capacity for fooling ourselves particularly in matters concerning our motives. What am I? Who am I? Where am I going? Have I any overriding purpose? We have a kind of a three-fold structure, the person we think we are, the person others think we are, and the person we really are. It is with this latter person we must come to grips and by the time we have pondered over some of these disturbing ideas we are ready to begin the task of fulfilling our lives. Frankl suggests that we begin by finding an overall Meaning for life, a kind of a general overriding purpose for living. Then there are lesser, but more individual Meanings; a Meaning in relationship to our work, a Meaning in relationship to other human beings, and above all a Meaning for our own personal and private affairs. The book goes into great detail in helping and explaining to us how to find these Meanings. I shall try to illustrate this by way of an example which must, perforce, be highly personal. The Meaning of my life at this very moment is to write these words that you are reading. It is evening and I would much prefer to run away from this task and go out to the pub for a drink with the lads, but if I do I will never get the work completed. So I must 'screw my courage to its sticking place' and finish the chapter I have set myself for today. In doing this I am finding a Meaning in life. Some other time when I go to the pub I can find a Meaning in life there too, by trying to make the evening as pleasant as I can for my companions. When I get home I can find a Meaning in life in my relationship with my family, by being tolerant and understanding towards all the foibles and complexities of family life. And so it goes on right through every aspect of living. The pursuit of Meaning is not the pursuit of perfection for perfection on its own is a cold and arid thing. Meaning involves love, a deep love for the whole principle of life and for every living thing, including ourselves. Perfection cannot give Meaning, but Meaning can give perfection.

Another important part of of the book deals with the matter of our attitudes towards events. We cannot change the facts of the past, we cannot undo the mistakes we have made, we cannot help unavoidable suffering or pain, but we can control the attitude we take up towards these events. We can either let them drag us down or learn a lesson from them which will help us in the future. As Fabry himself put it: 'Above all Meaning can be found in accepting the unavoidable and, by doing so, turning it into a challenge. History is full of examples supporting this view: a stutterer may resign or become a Demosthenes; a blind, deaf mute may despair or become a Helen Keller; a polio cripple may withdraw from life or become President of the United States.'

One other important lesson I learned from the book was this: We will never find the totality of Truth in this life but we can have many truthful enlightenments. We will not find the totality of Beauty either, but our lives can be enriched by many beautiful experiences. If our lives consist of a search for happiness we will fail hopelessly, but if instead we search for Meaning we will find happiness.

Dualla was still sailing steadily almost due south only slightly heeled over because the wind had about reached force three and after a short time I was in a position to lay Skiddy Island at the entrance to Castletownsend. Indeed this is a difficult island to pick out until you are right upon it as it seems to merge into the mainland behind. I put

Dualla about and headed her for harbour, and as I was sailing along I began to notice that the waves were ever so slowly getting bigger and bigger, much bigger than the strength of the wind warranted. This could mean only one thing: a storm was coming up. Out to sea perhaps five hundred miles a storm was blowing and moving towards Ireland. As the waves passed out of the storm area they kept moving at considerable speed to finally break upon our shores. But the storm could not be far behind. All this I learned from old Hare Island fishermen, and years later confirmed it in books on Oceanography. From May to October the Hares, as they were called, lobster fished the south coast from Cork to Mizen Head in their half-decked boats. They landed their catch once a week and spent the remainder of the time fishing and resting alternately, while at night they anchored in harbours or inlets, most of which were unknown to yachtsmen. Many of them could hardly read or write, nor had they ever heard a weather forecast, but there was little they did not know about the sea or storms. I looked at the barometer and sure enough it was dropping fast. I was glad that I was making for a safe and sheltered harbour.

I checked the sailing directions for Castletownsend and examined the chart so as to familiarise myself with the depths. One can never be too careful. We often delude ourselves that we remember everything from last year, but the older we get the less we remember. *The Sailing Directions for the South Coast of Ireland* are excellent and no yachtsman should be without a copy. They were written by the late Harry Donegan who made this guide his life's work, and since then thousands of yachtsmen have reason to thank him. I notice, with gladness, that my edition gratefully acknowledges his magnificent work. But with our usual curious mentality we had to go abroad to get someone to write a foreword. Or perhaps I am wrong, and it is fair exchange. Perhaps the forewords to all British sailing directions are written by Irishmen!

High Island really guards the entrance to Castletownsend,

and it presents the appearance of an old Irish *crannog* with little openings all around to let in the air and light. It has a collection of satellites with such orchestrated names as Low Island, Horse Island, Skiddy Island and Flea Island. What takes my fancy is that an island should be called after fleas. Belloc would have loved this which would have reminded him of his own 'fleas that tease in the high Pyrenees'.

Before long I found myself sailing past the little lantern —it is not a lighthouse—on Reen Point and then the whole beautiful vista of Castlehaven opened up with its luxuriant wooded shores and the little old-world village of Castletownsend itself nestling sideways in the bright green foliage. I started the engine, took off the foresail, let the main run free, and swung *Dualla* around into the wind. Here in two fathoms of water opposite the village I dropped anchor. Strangely enough it is when I come into harbour that I miss having companions, and this is entirely for a selfish reason. I now have to drop the anchor, take down and stow the sails, inflate the punt, launch it, scrub the decks and a dozen other little jobs that were always done for me before. However, by taking them all nice and easy, one after the other, I got them over with, while at the same time the remains of last nights stew was heating on the oven. Then with a bottle of wine, the bowl of the fricasse which I had put together, the tail-end of a fine bastable cake, I sat out on the deck to enjoy my meal, in the magnificent, breathtaking surroundings of this little haven of peace.

The village of Castletownsend is still part of another century. The new rich have not yet taken over, and the old rich are decaying with some dignity. From their ancient mansions they look eastwards across the sea to mother England and wistfully sigh for the days of long ago when they ruled the Irish people and were masters of the countryside. Castletownsend was originally owned by the O'Driscolls, a great Irish family who were once lords of West Cork. Their lands and castles were seized and given to an English planter named Townsend, from whom the village takes its name, and who in time established a colony of other planters on the lands of the dispossessed Irish. What happened in Castletownsend happened all over Ireland. The native Irish were mercilessly driven from their homes and farms to die of starvation on the roadside, if they had not already been butchered by the military. They were replaced largely by English soldiers, of lowly origin and mostly illiterate whose descendants are known today and have been for generations as the Ascendancy. Unlike the earlier Norman invaders who adopted the Irish language and customs, intermarried and became as Irish as the Irish themselves, the Ascendancy always regarded themselves as essentially English, and remained loyal to the English crown. This is one of the reasons why they failed so miserably as colonisers. Instead of ruling their territories in the interests of the people, they ruled them in the interests of a foreign power, and in this way built up against themselves an undying hatred. The aristocracy of France and Germany, for example, were completely French or German, and one has only to look at their great contribution to the world of art and culture to realise how truly national they were. In times of danger, they rallied to their country's cause, and thousands of them gave their lives on the battlefields of Europe for the honour of their nation and the safety of their people. How different the Ascendancy in Ireland. Most of them were too uneducated to make any contribution to native art and culture, and when the Irish nation needed them most, they rallied, not to their own country and to its people, but to the standard of the oppressor. Even as late as World War II when Ireland needed every man to defend her shores, they, with a few notable exceptions, deserted her, and joined the forces of a potential invader. All this is sad, but sadder still is the fact that in 1922, when Ireland regained her freedom they could have undone much of the damage of centuries. They could have thrown in their lot with the new nation and declared themselves Irish. They could have entered politics and public life and worked in the interests of the Irish people, and if they had only done so then they would now be one of the most powerful influences in the country.

But they missed this great opportunity, and today, as the Irish nation marches onwards, they sit in their crumbling mansions throughout Ireland bemoaning their lot in far back accents and drinking the health of a Crown and a nation who have long forgotten their very existence. Deserted by the English, ignored by the Irish people amongst whom they live, they have become figures of fun, without a country or without a rallying point—a pitiable exit for a class who could have become the leaven of the nation. I asked one of them why they allowed this state of things to come to pass, and his reply was understandable, and in a sense admirable, but pathetic in the light of events.

'We felt we would be letting down our co-religionists in the North if we co-operated with Republicans,' he explained rather sadly. 'But only now when it is too late have we seen our mistake.'

The wind was beginning to blow harder as I got the evening weather forecast, which gave force five to six for Fastnet and Shannon, but six to seven for Sole. I have found that very often what is in Sole today is in Fastnet tomorrow, and I also find that the Radio Eireann forecasts at 8 a.m. and 6 p.m. are better for Irish waters than the B.B.C. shipping forecasts. This only stands to reason since they are on the spot and have a great deal more experience of Irish weather conditions. But one thing puzzles me. They regularly refer to 'gale gusts in exposed places'. Now what in the hell is an 'exposed place'? I certainly do not know. Now I believe that in anything of force five or over a second anchor is called for, as one never knows how a rope may snap, or a link come loose and it's always safer to have an alternative. So I rowed out in the punt and dropped the fisherman's anchor, which together with the thirty-five pound C.Q.R. should hold *Dualla* in any kind of a blow.

I had had a few evenings 'out' since the cruise began and I now thought it was time to spend an evening at 'home' which meant an evening cleaning *Dualla*. It is astonishing how untidy and indeed dirty, a boat can become in a few days. The deck alone was well tattooed with the thanks-giving symbols of the seagulls and other birds that I fed in Glandore and along the way. The foredeck was coated with mud, which came off the anchor and chain and was now beginning to bake itself into the deck, and so after dinner I changed into overalls and with deck scrubber and bucket I worked hard on it for the best part of an hour and got it reasonably clean, but nothing like as clean as those decks I envy in ads in yachting magazines. It took me more than another two hours to tidy and clean the inside of the boat and then tired out I settled down for a good night's rest. The wind was now blowing hard, but I was safe and snug in a good anchorage and soon was lulled to sleep by the thunderous roar of the Atlantic beating against the rocks and cliffs outside the sheltered harbour.

In the morning the sun was shining but the wind was still blowing hard sending the clouds tearing through a clear blue sky. After breakfast I rowed across the harbour to the little pier at Raheen and strolled along the cliffs out to Reen Point from where I had a perfect view of the wide turbulent ocean. As far out as the horizon the raging sea was a mass of white foam and it seemed to shake the whole coast as each monstrous growling wave crashed hundreds of tons of water against the land. It was awe-inspiring but by no meaning frightening. It is not too hard to understand why our ancestors worshipped the sea, for in my first moments on the cliff some primitive instinct made me want to go down on my knees and pay homage to this savage powerful force. I sat there for nearly an hour spell-bound by the wild unrest, and thinking how much of the beautiful shoreline scenery of Ireland we owe to storms. If there were no storms our coastline would be flat and dull like the banks of a canal, just as if there were no suffering in life we would all be morons. There is a meaning behind everything if we could only find it. As I walked back along to the pier the contrast was remarkable. Outside the enor-mous waves lashed with wild fury while in the shelter of the harbour they were just frolicking little ripples scarcely disturbing the boats at anchor. I rowed over to the village because I wanted to visit St Barrahane's graveyard where the mortal remains of Edith Somerville and Violet Martin, better known as Somerville and Ross, rest. To get to the churchyard you walk up a narrow lane with overhanging trees. The scent of wild woodbine, cowslip and lilac fills the air. The humming of the bees and the twittering of the birds welcome you. You climb up fifty-two steps, one for each week of the year, past the tombs of great families to the very highest point where in the shadow of stately palm trees the two writers rest side by side united in their love for all eternity. Edith Somerville seems to have been a man in every sense of the word except the biological. She formed a deep relationship with her cousin, Violet Martin, from Rosscahill in Galway, who eventually came to live with Edith in Castletownsend, and together they wrote several books which brought them some fame in the world of letters in the early years of this century. They were not great writers but they had an ability, and from the several books that they wrote two stand out as having considerable merit, viz. *The Real Charlotte* and *The Big House at Inver*. In these two novels they were writing about a class they knew intimately, their own class, the Ascendancy, and they succeeded in giving a first rate portrayal of that upper-crust world. I believe that on these two novels will rest their claim to fame. As for their numerous other works, such as *The Irish R.M. Stories*, they are hardly worth a second thought. Here they tried to deal with a theme which was utterly beyond them—a theme involving the ordinary Irish people about which they knew very little and understood even less. In their eyes the Irish were the lower orders destined by God to be kept in ignorance and poverty, while the Ascendancy were firmly in the saddle and ruled by divine right. The fruits of the earth were to be theirs, while the droppings and the swill was for the Irish. Somerville and Ross never saw themselves in any other light and their writings were mostly an attempt to portray to a civilised folk, namely the genteel English sipping afternoon tea with the vicar, the goings-on of a race of ignorant half-savages. They presented the unfortunate oppressed Irish peasant, dressed in rags through no fault of his own as a 'be jaysus, begorra, top-of-the-morning-to-you' character whose main traits were dishonesty, laziness and comic stupidity. They completely missed the reality that the poor Irish peasant who acted like that towards them did so because he was starving, because he was expected to do so in order to get a few shillings or a meal, but deep in his simple heart he hated and dispised them. Remember the haunting cry of the great Irish poet Egan O'Rahilly (translated by Frank O'Connor), who was reduced to destitution and had to beg from one of the Ascendancy, Valentine Brown.

That my old bitter heart was pierced in this black doom
That foreign devils have made our land a tomb,
That the sun that was Munster's glory has gone down
Has made me a beggar before you, Valentine Brown

Somerville and Ross could have achieved a lasting literary fame had they come down from their magnificent hunters and tried to understand the Irish, espoused their cause, shared their joys and sorrows, plumbed the depths of their souls, and saw them for what they were, a proud intelligent people, with thousands of years of culture behind them, just emerging from centuries of slavery into the light of a freedom which was almost upon them. These unfortunate people were given expression by other writers of Ascendancy background like Synge, Yeats, Lady Gregory, who unlike Somerville and Ross, were sensitive to the great national drama which was about to unfold itself. Somerville and Ross lacked this sensitivity and the great literary renaissance which was sweeping the country passed over their heads. Not only did they lack this sensitivity which is the hallmark of all great writers, but they were priggish to the point of stupidity. They would have no dealings with the great Irish writers of the period because to do so would be offensive to Violet's brother who was a staunch and professional Unionist. They were outraged at Yeats' love for Maud Gonne. How could a great poet love such a traitor to the Crown? De Valera was an unspeakable cad. Once Edith met Michael Collins, sadly enough on the day of his death, but it was only to demand that he keep 'the murderers and ruffians' away from their sheltered home and village. Somerville and Ross as writers are now moving into the land of oblivion and as soon as the remnants of those who like to read about the buffoonery of Paddy the Irishman are dead and gone Somerville and Ross will be forgotten. The younger generation, even those with Ascendancy background, are much too intelligent and appreciative of good literature to have any time for them.

In many ways all this is a great pity. They could write well and had greatness within their grasp, but perhaps their prejudices were too entrenched, too deeply embedded, ever to be moved. Yet strangely their private lives were anything but orthodox. Edith had a profound distaste for the opposite sex, and after one abortive attempt to form an alliance with a female relation she remained alone and unattached for five years until she met and loved Violet Martin, who was to be her companion in death as well as in life. Edith and Violet found themselves to be twin souls and believed that by a fusion of their souls through love, each could find fulfilment in life. For twenty-five wonderful years their existence was one existence in common. They lived and worked together, producing book after book, in a state as near to perfect harmony as could be found. But the terrible law of life is that this harmony, this contentment, this near-happiness does not last. And Edith's world was torn asunder when in 1915, at the height of their relationship, Violet died. Day by day as Edith sat by the bedside watching the life ebb away from her beloved, she felt her own soul fade and die with her. It was during those tragic poignant hours that she sketched the head of the dying Violet, a sketch of such rare beauty and delicacy that it could command a place in any gallery anywhere in the world. When Violet's body was committed to the grave, at the very spot where I was standing, Edith left the little churchyard and wandered alone through the fields and haunts where she had so often roamed with her dead beloved, finding in the beauty of the countryside balm for her wounded heart. Death may end a life, but it does not end a relationship of love. Edith lived on for another thirty years, but because she felt herself so united to Violet, even in death, she still published all her books under the name of Somerville and Ross. Edith lived to a great old age, and when she died she was buried, by her own request, side by side with the woman she loved. Rupert Brooke could have written their epitaph:

These hearts were woven of human joys and cares
Washed marvellously with sorrow, swift to mirth
The years had given them kindness, Dawn was theirs,
And sunset, and the colours of the earth.

These have seen movement, and heard music; known
Slumber and waking, loved; gone proudly friended;
Felt the quick air of wonder; sat alone;
Touched furs and flowers and cheers, All this is ended.

There are waters blown by changing winds to laughter
And lit by the rich skies, all day. And after,
Frost, with a gesture, stays the waves that dance
And wandering loveliness. He leaves a white
Unbroken glory, a gathered radiance,
A width, a shining peace, under the night.

5

Like most summer storms this one died down during the night and I awoke next morning to hear the splash of oars, the rattle of pulleys, the throb of engines. After their enforced idleness the lobster-men were getting ready to put out to sea and gather its rich harvest. I enjoyed a leisurely breakfast as usual in the cockpit, and then cleared *Dualla's* decks for action. I stowed the punt, hoisted the sails, broke out the anchors cursed the fact that I had no one to help me, and then headed for the open sea.

There is a narrow passage just at the entrance to the harbour, between Horse Island and the mainland, which I would like to have gone through for no other reason than that it would be great to be able to boast that I had sailed through a sound with the strangest name on the Irish coast viz. Flea Sound. I once asked an old fisherman over a pint how it came to get that peculiar name.

'You see,' he said, 'there's a strange kind of grass growing on Horse Island that can cure the scour in horses and in the ould days the people used to swim their animals across so that they could eat the grass and get cured. Nearly every day there would be people from all over West Cork coming with their horses hoping to make them well again, and on the way across the water was so cowld and salty that the fleas left the horses and tried to swim for their dear life. In my grandfather's day I often saw millions of fleas half-drowned on the shore, but it doesn't happen at all now since people got vets to cure the scour, and the fleas can live at their ease. All that belongs to the ould times. They tell me it started with a fellow called Finn MacCool, but that must have been a long time ago, for my grandfather did not remember him.' The twinkle in his eye assured me that he had told a fine whopper, but it was a good story and I did not begrudge him the pint. Fleas are not affected by water. I remember once carrying out an experiment with a flea-catcher friend of mine. We put a live flea into a glass of water and left him there for a week. We then drained off the water and put the flea on a piece of cardboard out in the sun; after a few minutes he sprang to life and hopped merrily away none the worse for his adventure. Fleas, like politicians, are very flexible and adaptable beings. It was Swift who wrote that pithy quatrain which, in its way, is the best description I know of politicians:

> Big fleas have little fleas
> Upon their backs to bit them
> Little fleas have lesser fleas
> And so ad infinitum.

As I sailed out into the wild freshness of the morning sea I could not help thinking of poor tormented Swift who spent the summer of 1723 sailing up and down this coast trying to find rest for his weary spirit and balm for his wounded heart after the death of Vanessa. Once when he was stormbound in Castlehaven he wrote a long poem in Latin called *Carbery Rocks* inspired by the wild Atlantic waves dashing against the headlands.

It is a heavy ponderous dreary poem, but Swift himself thought it was a masterpiece and classed it as one of his greatest compositions. Maybe when we create or compose something under great sorrow it lives long in the memory and we give it an exaggerated importance. Swift was a mediocre poet but a truly great writer of prose. He was the voice of Ireland in his time. He spoke for the poor, the hungry, the crippled, the old, who had nobody else to defend them and he lacerated with all the strength at his command the obtuseness and smugness of the Establishment of his day who were only too happy to crush, oppress and starve thousands so that they could continue their gracious and genteel living. Most of his poetry is more gentle, more subdued, as if another side of his nature were expressing itself. On one occasion he was travelling towards Dublin when a violent thunderstorm arose and he ran under an old tree for shelter. He was soon joined by a young couple also sheltering from the storm. The young girl was obviously pregnant and the man explained that they were walking to Dublin to get married before the child was born. Swift introduced himself and suggested that to spare them the journey he could marry them there and then. They agreed and Swift performed the ceremony. When the storm had abated and they were leaving the young man asked Swift for some marriage lines to prove they were man and wife. Swift wrote rapidly on a piece of paper and gave it to them. They thanked him, for they could not read. What he wrote was:

> Under an oak, in stormy weather
> I joined this rogue and whore together
> And none but he who rules the thunder
> Can put this rogue and whore asunder.

As I looked at the beautiful coast of Cork, with its majestic cliffs and jagged rocks I realised that what I now saw was exactly what Swift saw more than two hundred and fifty years ago. Nothing had changed. The coast of Cork lives on. It is only we who die.

The wind was blowing against me from the south-west so I had to take a long tack out to sea until I was almost level with Cape Clear Island and then put *Dualla* about to make a straight run for the entrance to Baltimore Harbour. It was another glorious day and the whole panorama of enchanting islands and mountains from the far Mizen Head opened up as if to welcome me. All apprehension had now gone for in this magical corner of Ireland I felt completely at home. I passed close up to the sharp peaks of the Stag Rocks on my first tack and just at the edge of the water two beautiful young seals were besporting themselves in the summer sunlight. When they saw me coming they disappeared into the blue sea and I thought they were gone. But no. They surfaced quite near *Dualla*, their beautiful little heads smiling up at me. They circled around the boat and followed curiously for about two or three minutes and then disappeared far under the sea again.

Seals are amongst the most intelligent creatures in the

world. They have a remarkably powerful brain and they are gifted with a wisdom and understanding seldom found in the general run of animals. Seals are very easily tamed and are capable of a great love for and attachment to man. There is a story told about a West Cork farmer in the early years of this century who had a pet seal whose name was Buttons. Buttons was a delightful loving companion for the children, gentle, playful and bubbling over with life. During the day he occupied himself up and down the sea shore and frolicked to his heart's content with the dogs, cats and other domestic animals. At night he slept under the little bed of the farmer's five year old daughter whose special pet he was. Then one winter the farmer's cattle began to get sick from a seemingly incurable disease and many of them died. In those superstitious days there was an old hag living near-by who had the reputation of having second sight, so the farmer consulted her about his cattle, and this imposter told him that he would have to get rid of the seal if he wanted his cattle to be cured. The stupid lout believed her and one morning before his little daughter got up he sailed out beyond the Fastnet, threw the seal into the Atlantic, and returned home. He was hardly inside the door when Buttons appeared behind him, and shrieking with delight, jumped into bed with the little girl. The farmer consulted the old hag again, and she told him that it would be un-lucky to kill the seal, but that he should gouge out his two eyes, so that he could not see, and dump him into the ocean again. The imbecile performed this savage act on the sea shore so that his little daughter could not hear the pain-ful scream of poor Buttons, and once again brought him out to sea. The little girl was distraught when she missed her pet and cried almost non-stop for three days. Then one night a wild storm blew up from the south-west and high seas lashed the shore. At dawn there came a series of unmerciful piercing wails from outside the door. The little girl looked out and saw Buttons. She ran downstairs, opened the door, only to see him flapping his way towards the shore. She ran after him as she was, in her nightie, and followed him as he climbed uneasily to the top of a tall rock. Just as she put her arms around him he slid into the raging sea, bringing her along with him. Three days later they found the bodies of the little girl and the blinded seal washed up on the shore. There was a look of radiant happiness about her face.

I did not notice the time slipping by until I found myself with the Gaiscanaun Sound almost abeam so I put *Dualla* about and set course for the large white beacon guarding the entrance to Baltimore harbour. The islands of Carbery were popping up one by one out of the sea, Cape Clear, the Calves, Sherkin, Hare, Long Island and many others; islands which are now largely deserted but which once rang loud with life, joy and laughter. In the old days they were peopled by the farmer-fisherman inhabitant, that is one who farmed a little and fished a little dependant on the weather and the seasons of the year. A few pounds could also be picked up from time to time piloting ships into Crookhaven, Schull or Baltimore. There was once a Caper who was taken on board a coaster as a pilot and the captain wishing to make sure that the man knew what he was about asked him to 'box the compass'. This meant to recite the points, and quarter points from north through to south and north again both clockwise and anti-clockwise. The Caper could not do it and was about to be dismissed when his cunning prompted him to lie to the captain that he had very little English but could do it in Irish.

'Let's hear you,' said the captain. The Caper knew enough to know that the words should follow suit such as, north, north by east, north-north-east etc. and that the captain would be sure to spot the similarity of sounds in any language, so the Caper shouted out slowly in the Irish language, 'My grandfather, my grandfather's mother, my grandfather's grandmother, my grandfather's great grandmother. . .'

'Enough,' said the Captain. 'I have wronged you my good man. Take charge of the ship.' And so the happy Caper earned his fiver.

The people of the islands lived in a world well removed from the inhabitants of the mainland. They were a simpler people and lived closer to nature, and most of them only left their island homes a few times a year to attend fairs or to do some seasonal shopping. A bishop was once administering Confirmation in Schull and in the course of his examination asked a lad from Long Island how many Gods there were. 'Great and holy priest,' replied the lad who was on the mainland for the first time and who was deeply impressed with the vastness of what he saw. 'In Long Island we have only one God but 'tis likely that in this big world over here that there could be a lot more.' He was put back for further instruction. They had a rather strict moral code and I'm told on reliable authority that it was only towards the end of the last century that the first illegitimate child was born on Hare Island. It happened to a girl who had been in service on the mainland and when the child was born they were both banished to Ireland by unanimous wish of the islanders. Decent enough, however, they gave her a stocking full of money and a boat laden with food and clothing to get her started in her new life. But all that world of the past is now gone and bit by bit the islands are being deserted. On Cape Clear there are only about two hundred people left out of what was once more than a thousand. Like the moths who rush to the flame which will destroy them, they rush to the cities on the mainland and leave behind them the ruins of the little homesteads, and the gaunt skeletons of their decaying boats in sheltered nooks on the seashore. Their places are now being taken on many of the islands by drop-outs from the cities to whom you and I give a portion of our hard-earned money in the form of dole to keep them in comfort and idleness. I once asked an old inhabitant if these well-paid blow-ins would not work and try to cultivate the islands.

'Work?' he asked in amazement. 'They wouldn't be seen in the same house as a shovel.'

Dualla was on self-steering as she headed towards Baltimore. The time passed as I lay there in the cockpit, my feet resting on the combing, reading a little from a book of poetry and thinking a little on what I had read and all the time the day-dreams left my mind and seemed to go dancing on the glistening surface of the sea. Then the cry of a seagull, the flash of a shoal of mackerel, the dive of a gannet would drag me back to reality again, but only to release me once more to those wonderful crazy, fleeting dreams that can take a man totally out of himself and transpose him into the eternal. The whole face of the sea had a soft radiance, tender and beautiful as seas sometimes have after storms. The wild rugged coastline stood out transfigured against the bright clear sky, no longer the scene of savage fury but of peaceful calm. Nature has few things more beautiful to show than a blue sea breaking against cliffs and rocks and swirling back again in white streams of foam, for every moment you expect to see beautiful mermaids coming upwards from a fairy world, and as you listen to the sound of the waves breaking gently against the side of the boat, you feel quite sure you are only one step from Paradise.

There is something very majestic about the entrance to Baltimore harbour. Tall cliffs raise their sublime forms up from the lapping sea making a kind of portal which leads you into a large expanse of ever-widening water not too unlike a sheltered inland lake. Almost every time I come here I get the same kind of welcome which takes the form of a cold squall that blusters down from under the lighthouse on Sherkin Island and sure enough it did not fail me this time. As I was heading for the black buoy which marks the Loo rock an almighty squall hit *Dualla* and fairly well heeled her over on her side. I could not luff up here as to do so would put me on the rocks of the island, so I eased the main and spilled the wind and so came up on an even keel once more. I sailed her on towards the Walter Scott buoy, then headed her into the wind and dropped the main, and anchored in one-and-a-half fathoms of water a cable or so south-west of the pier. When I had the sails tidied, the punt launched, the anchor firmly secured I sat back in the cockpit, with a tumbler of wine in my hand basking in and enjoying the blue magnificence of the sunlit harbour. Later I rowed ashore, went into a pub where I met John Willie Nolan and together over a flagon of ale we-settled the affairs of the world.

Baltimore was to be my half-way resting place so I stay-ed there almost a week making excursions each day in the punt to one or other of the many beautiful islands within easy range of where *Dualla* was anchored. Sherkin was my first call and it was as beautiful as ever. When you ramble along its dusty fuschia-covered bohereens, where scarcely a sound can be heard except the humming of bees play-fully tantalising the hearts of the flowers, you feel in a real sense that you have touched the limit of time. I strolled at my ease across the island and called in to say a prayer in the little church on the hill, where everything was hushed and silent except for the rhythmic tick-tock of an old timepiece on the wall. Little country churches, unlike the spiritual supermarkets of the cities and towns, have an atmosphere about them that makes it easy for one to meditate and to pray. In this they surpass the great and mighty cathedrals, which owe their existence to the vanity and ego-mania of some man of power.

When I was leaving the church I remembered a story Mike Donoghue once told me about a time during the war when, on account of rationing and bad weather, the people and animals on Sherkin were starving with the hunger. The bell rope on the church was a *sugán* made from the very best of hay and a randy young bullock was passing one day and I suppose saw no reason why the good hay should go to waste, so he proceeded to eat the rope. This caused the bell to ring feverishly and the islanders thought the country was being invaded by the English or the Germans. All the women knelt down around the firesides to say the rosary and pray for peace, while the men collected pitch-forks, ash plants and shot-guns and assembled at the Abbey strand to repel the panzers. When it was found out what really caused the bell to ring there was an adjournment to the local pub

82

and a right good time was had by all for the rest of the evening. Of course Mike did not expect me to believe that story no more than he'd expect me to believe the words of a song, nor no more than he expected me to believe another story he told me with a twinkle in his eye about a Sherkin fisherman who was out fishing all day and only caught a small eel. He came home late in the evening very hungry, cut a skelp of bacon from a side hanging out of the rafters and together with a couple of duck eggs and the eel he threw the lot on the frying pan over the fire. He went out to milk the goat and when he came back the eel had eaten the bacon and eggs and thus well fortified made an escape back to the sea through a hole in the corner of the half-door for letting the chickens in and out.

Most yachtsmen and seafaring visitors to Baltimore over the past fifty years will remember Mike Donoghue. He had become something of an institution. His small frail figure, Kitchener moustache and weather-beaten face, rowing in his tiny punt was a familiar sight throughout the long summer days. When I first met Mike several years ago he was already a very old man; how old exactly he was not too sure himself. We became close friends immediately and the honour was mine, for he was one of the kindest and most sincere and most honest men I have ever met. His years at sea made him a silent man with little to say but if he accepted you as a friend he spoke freely in poetic words of wit and wisdom. I never found out whether he could read or write, but it was of little importance anyhow. The most cultured kings and leaders of Ireland's golden age knew little of the alphabet and they were none the worse for that. Time and again I sat with him on the high cliffs over Baltimore just looking out to the horizon exchanging sea-lore and chatting about ships and seamanship of bygone days. He was free with his counsel, advice and example and I can thank him for a lot of what I know about the sea. When he died they buried him in the beautiful little grave-yard overlooking Church strand. There, with the sound of the waves and the call of the gulls filling the still calm air, his mortal remains await entry into the final and safest Harbour of all.

I strolled along towards the western end of the island and the beautiful silver beaches, with a wilderness of sand, that open up to the great waves of the Atlantic. I rested myself under a clamp of purple heather on a small hill overlooking the strand. The July sun poured down its pleasant rays on dozens of light frocks, flimsy bikinis, naked backs and bronzed faces of young and old as they lay in quiet nooks and corners along the edge of the sea. The married couples were sitting with their backs to each other, reading or dozing, in that terrible slavery where every word and gesture can be anticipated; the very old seemed to find renewed youth and joy building forts and raths and castles with their grandchildren; and the young hippies lay caressing each other's bodies with tingling strokes of desire. Some say that permissiveness is the big characteristic of the present age. But I wonder? A synod of bishops in the eleventh century condemned the hippies in that day: 'They go about naked in public, lie in bake ovens, frequent taverns, games, harlots, earn their bread by their vices, so that no hope of their amendment remaineth'. Youth's rebellion against orthodoxy is as old as man himself. As I gazed down at those beautiful breasts, well-shaped thighs and thoroughbred ankles I could not help feeling that I might be much better off if I had a woman to share my days and nights instead of going through life alone. To my surprise, for the past six years a lot of my friends thought likewise and were kind enough to invite me to discreet dinner parties at which there was always one unattached female. By a coincidence I invariably found myself sitting beside her, and in this unusual way I met some of the nicest women a man could ask to meet in the running of his days. A few of them, having given the matter some consideration, thought I was worth a second look, and they were kind enough to meet me again, but somehow or another I just failed to make the grade and one by one they dropped me in the kindest possible way. One was more forthright than the rest. 'What woman wants to spend her life with you?' she asked. 'A man who has little interest in money, position or fame and who has no ambition to do anything other than live and enjoy each day as it comes. Any normal woman needs to go out into the world, to dress herself up in a beautiful way, and to meet her friends and acquaintances at dances, dinners and parties. How could she be happy with you, who most of the time prefers the company of animals to human beings, who even boasted that in the most glittering social occasions you could see nothing more than a collection of potential corpses, and who given the choice of spending an evening with a lord in his castle or a tinker in his tent, would choose the tent. A woman wants normality in her life — not a crackpot like you.' I have to admit that I agreed with her and indeed I commended her on her honesty. Anyway my children tell me that at my age, no woman wants me, and that I should be saying the Rosary twice a day and doing the Holy Hour once a week for the good of my soul. All the same I wouldn't mind laying down on the silver strand of Sherkin with a beautiful girl in a bikini and maybe she wouldn't mind if I tickled her now and then behind the ear with a feather from the tail of a seagull. We could always say the Rosary afterwards.

As I was sitting there enjoying the sun a young bearded hippie and his girl friend lay down on the strand not far away and got to work without undue delay. The girl stretched herself out in a bikini while he commenced to tickle the exposed parts of her body with the tip of his beard. Nearby sat a middle-aged woman, her hair tied in a bun, the varicose veins on her legs looking like the tributaries of the Amazon on a coloured map of South America. She was knitting some kind of a garment and when she saw the carry-on of the two lovers she began to mutter a lot of incoherent words the only ones of which I could catch were: . . .'disgrace. . . revolting. . . disgusting. . . Catholic country. . .' The more she muttered the more feverishly she knitted and after a while she gathered up her trappings and departed still muttering. The thought crossed my mind that her name could be Madame Defarge, and the only thing missing was the guillotine.

As I strolled back towards the Abbey Pier and *Dualla* I remembered an incident that happened long long ago when I was a young officer in the army. I had a friend who was truly the ugliest man I ever saw. He looked so like an animal that his ability to stand on his hind legs was always a source of wonderment and mystery to me, but despite all this he was the Don Juan *cum honoris* of the century. No matter where he went he could have whatever woman he wanted to in spite of competition from the handsomest of men. Once, when we both had a few more drinks than we should have had, he heeded my urgent pleadings and told me his secret.

'I know I'm no Clark Gable,' he explained. 'Indeed I'm more like the Hunchback of Notre Dame. But looks or age don't matter with a woman if you can capture her imagination. When I set my eye on a woman I first of all get her talking about herself. So long as a woman is so doing she is never bored. I flatter her about her beauty and intelligence. She knows she's more beautiful than I am so to encourage her I let her think she's more intelligent, also. Then I arrange an accidental meeting near a bar or hotel when she's on her way home from work and we have a drink or a cup of coffee. I encourage her to talk more about herself but I never make an amorous suggestion or put a finger on her. A woman responds better to a man's physical indifference than to his attentions. She doesn't really want me — what she wants is that I should want her. I am always a bit mysterious about myself and I leave her each time with a growing sense of curiosity. Sometimes I throw a paradox into the conversation. I tell her that she's like all women but that no woman is like her. Most women are too stupid to grasp that but it sounds good and she doesn't know whether its flattery or not. Then when I judge that the time is ripe I invite her out one evening to a nice romantic restaurant for dinner. During the meal I begin to quote little bits of poetry, particularly nature poetry to her. All women love Wordsworth, Blake, Keats and particularly

Joyce Kilmer's *Trees*. Wasn't it Keats himself who said that most women would like to be married to a poem? Then at the coffee stage when I judge I have her intellectually captured I tell her how attracted I am by her and how much I would like to have something deeper and more permanent between us but unfortunately this can never be. At this point I pause to light a cigarette and take a furtive look around the restaurant. Her curiosity has now reached maddening point. Then I slowly tell her, almost with tears in my eyes, that I am a homosexual. I continue quickly to tell her how much I would like to be orientated towards women but so far no woman has been able to break through despite my goodwill. I don't have to say any more. Within a week she will have seduced, if not raped, me. It always works. The woman is not born yet who can resist converting a homosexual to the normal ways of women. Try it,' he concluded. 'You cannot fail.'

In my innocence I tried it. She was a bewitching redhead, with long graceful legs, breasts that were forever bouncing and eyes at once inviting and provocative. I followed his instructions to the letter. I had prepared myself for the *grand finale* by learning the words of Joyce Kilmer's *Trees* as well as a few other poems which I hoped would touch her heart. The setting was perfect — an old barn-type restaurant with turf fire, stone floor and candlelight. After I recited *Trees* there was a slight mist visible in her eyes but after Tennyson's *Tears Idle Tears* I could see she had surrendered completely. I now moved in for the kill. In slow halting words, that would have done justice to Anew Mac-Master, I delivered myself of the speech I had prepared:

'I hope you will not be offended at what I have to say to you,' I said. 'For some time past I feel we have both come very close to each other and it is my dearest wish that we should come still closer so that we might strengthen and deepen our relationship into something beautiful and lasting. But sadly there is one big obstacle.' Here I slowly lit a cigarette and glanced round the dimly-lit room, with a sad thoughtful face, as instructed. 'I could only tell this to you,

I continued. 'I am a homosexual.'

Her whole face lit up as if by magic. Her eyes seemed to dance with joy.

'Wonderful! Wonderful!' she exclaimed, taking my hands in hers. 'That's absolutely wonderful! We can have a fantastic time together. You see, I'm a lesbian.'

I have never, never tried that approach again.

The Ilen river, which is tidal, empties itself into the ocean between Hare Island and Sherkin and one of the most delightful trips I made was to row the punt a few miles upstream to the wooded island of Inisbeg. I went with the last two hours of a strong flood tide barely touching the oars to give her way and direction. On my way I passed close to Quarantine Island, which is littered, beneath the surface and undergrowth, with dead men's bones. In the olden days no ship was allowed to land its cargo in Baltimore or Skibbereen if there were any cases of a contagious disease on board. So an unfortunate sufferer was unceremoniously dumped on Quarantine Island and in most cases left there to die. The peace and tranquility surrounding it today is a far cry from those inhuman times when the moans of the dying echoed through the surrounding countryside. The land on both sides of the river falls steeply to the shore, and the colourful mixture of golden whin and purple heather makes it look like the road to fairyland. Inisbeg itself is a dream island, although it is not strictly speaking an island since it is connected to the mainland by a bridge. It is one of those romantic settings which make the heart throb with yearnings never to leave but remain there to the end of one's days. It was here on Inisbeg that Kay Summersby, who was Eisenhower's driver during World War II, was born. Kay and Ike formed a deep attachment to one another and their love affair was one of the most closely guarded secrets of the war. It was not that the security men were unduly worried about the effect this would have on the morals of the British or American soldiers, but they were rather terrified that the Germans would get wind of it and this would give Goebbels a first class scandal to broadcast to the world and thus make a major propaganda score. As it turned out this secrecy was all rather a waste of time for the Germans knew every detail of the affair but they chose not to make use of it since the private lives of some of their own top brass were not above reproach and they feared Allied retaliation. Immediately the war was over Eisenhower wrote to General Marshall and told him that he wanted to divorce Mamie, his wife, and marry Kay. Marshall wrote back angrily threatening that if this happened he would smash Eisenhower for ever. Eisenhower, perhaps because of his political ambitions, backed down and dropped Kay. Later, before Truman left office he decently enough took all the correspondence out of the official state files and sent it to Eisenhower, saying that this was a personal matter and should not be left in the U.S. war archives.

Having spent more than an hour meandering around Inisbeg, wondering if it were really Shangri-la, I rowed back with the ebb tide but this time I took a turning to port at Jermy Reach and I landed first on Jones Island and then on Spanish Island. This island hopping of mine had a purpose. It was part of a search for something which I never found.

For centuries there was a traditional enmity between Waterford and Baltimore and more than once each made forays, always from the sea, into the other's territory. An old manuscript in Marsh's Library describes one such raid in the last century against the O'Driscolls led by a Pierce Dobbyn of Waterford, who, judging by his surname, could hardly have come from the Deices Gaeltacht. Part of the manuscript says:

Near to Inisherkin was an island called Inchipite, where Fineen O'Driscoll had his most pleasant seat in a castle adjoining to a hall, with an orchard and grove, all which they destroyed and razed to the earth, and from thence they entered into another island and burnt all the villages of the same. On Tuesday in Passion Week, one,

William Grant was on top of one of the castles, which being all on fire under him he stood upon one of the pinnacles and cried for help. One, Bulter, tied a small cord to an arrow and shot it up to Grant, at which he drew up a hawser fastened to the cord, and fixing the hawser to the pinnacle slid down and was received by his fellows on beds. After this, on Good Friday, the army arrived safe at Waterford.

What I have been searching for is this mysterious Inchipite, with its castle, hall and playgrounds. I walked almost every inch of Hare Island, The Skeames, Reenmore, The Calves, in fact every habitable island within reasonable distance of Sherkin. I once thought it might be the island on Lough Hyne where Fineen O'Driscoll died, but the manuscript says: 'near to Sherkin' and Lough Hyne is ten or twelve miles away. Once I thought I had found it when I came across a romantic sheltered lagoon on the Eastern Calf, with steep rocks on either side and connected to the sea by a long narrow passage only a few yards wide. But there was not a sign of any ancient buildings of any kind on any part of the island. This island is also so bare and windswept that I doubt if a tree or grove could survive. I asked several of the older generation in the area but to no avail. Even Mike Donoghue himself could not help me. The only other person I know who searched for the island was that grand old scholar and expert on the archaeology of West Cork, John T. Collins. He told me that it was a kind of a weekend pleasure palace with beautifully laid out gardens and arbours and spacious swimming pools like the magnificent baths of ancient Rome. This was normal amongst well-to-do Irish chieftains at that time, and quite an important part of such an establishment was a number of young attractive girls available to comfort the tired and war-weary nobles. But John T. died without ever being able to pinpoint exactly which island. I can still hear his hearty laughter when I told him how I could imagine the ageing Fineen besporting himself in the swimming pool like a frolicksome old shark giving chase to his shoal of nymphs, and then crossing over to the Franciscan Abbey founded by his family in Sherkin, to do penance and give liberal presents of gold to the monks. To have a foot in each camp, to make the best of both worlds has been one of man's deepest ambitions, and it seems as if many of the old Irish chieftains came near to realising it. Anyhow nobody has yet found the remains of this love-nest and perhaps it is just as well. The men of the past are entitled to their secrets and we should not ask too many questions. It would be a major disaster if it were discovered by some German or Dutch millionaire who would no doubt rebuild and develop it, and bring over a bevy of accomplished popsies from Hamburg and Amsterdam for the joy and delectation of the farmers of West Cork.

Coming towards the end of this short interlude in Baltimore my daughter Mary joined me for a few days and together with two young and beautiful Dutch girls, and two equally lovely Swedish girls who were attending the Baltimore Sailing School, we made many day trips in *Dualla* to the neighbouring harbours, inlets and bays. When the time for me to leave was drawing near I felt really sad at the thought of being alone again. Those few beautiful days in such winsome female company were so happy and carefree that I looked forward with a heavy heart to the next lonely phase of my journey. But I was not going to be entirely alone. Mary had brought my favourite dog, Maxie, from Cork and he was going to stay with me for the rest of the cruise. Let me introduce him to you. Maxie is a half-Alsatian, half Husky, loveable if he trusts you and dangerous if he doesn't. He combines some savage traits together with the serene wisdom of a philosopher. Of course he is much closer to me than many human beings. He has never betrayed me, never told me a lie, never passed off a dud cheque on me, or stolen money from my wallet, or gone around to his friends and told them that I was a stark raving but uncertified lunatic. If I listed all the nasty things human beings have done to me during the course of my life I could truthfully say that he has not done even one of them. At home he sleeps on the foot of my bed and at eight o'clock sharp every morning he rubs his rich furry head gently against my face to awaken me. He does the same when we sleep on *Dualla*—at the same time every morning and in the same way. He has sailed many times before so he is used to the ways of the sea. I was overjoyed that he could be with me for the rest of the cruise and so a day later when the morning sun threw its brilliant light on the rippling waters of the bay, we upped anchor, hoisted sail and slipped quietly out of Baltimore harbour.

6

My next port of call was Cape Clear Island and as the wind was blowing lightly from the North-West I set my course for South Harbour. Since the prevailing winds blow from the South or South-West, North Harbour is the one most frequently used, but it is very small, narrow with no room to anchor so that one must tie up alongside. This presents problems as it is only at the very end of the pier that there is adequate water and one must be constantly shunting and shifting to make way for the Mail Boat and other ferries which come and go regularly. South Harbour on the other hand is a delightful anchorage, with plenty of room but it can only be used in Northerly or Westerly winds as it is completely exposed to the South.

As I cleared the entrance to Baltimore I passed the famous Eastern Hole where the raider ships anchored during the Sack of Baltimore in 1631. Nearly everyone remembers from school days the beautiful poem by Thomas Davis:

The Summer sun is falling soft on Carbery's hundred isles
The Summer sun is gleaming still through Gabriel's rough
   defiles
Old Inisherkin's crumbled fane looks like a moulting bird
And in a calm and easy swell, the ocean tide is heard.
The hookers lie upon the beach; the children cease their play
The gossips leave the little inn; the house-holds kneel to pray;
And full of love and peace and rest—its daily labour o'er—
Upon that cosy creek there lay the town of Baltimore.

Here you have a picture of a perfectly peaceful happy Irish community at the end of the day. Davis goes on to describe the eerie silence of nightfall, a silence with a sense of forboding, and the two ships barely visible on the horizon. Long after darkness, when everyone was deep in slumber there is sudden turmoil:

A stifled gasp! a dreamy noise, 'The roof is in a flame'
From out their beds, and to their doors, rush maid and sire
   and dame.
And meet, upon the threshold stone, the gleaming sabres fall,
And over each black and bearded face the white and
   crimson shawl,
The yell of 'Allah' breaks above the prayer and shriek and
   roar
Oh, blessed God! the Algerine is Lord of Baltimore.

The two ships seen out to sea at dusk were Algerian pirates bent on a mission of capturing men and women to be used as slaves in Algeria. In a few hours all was over. The village was reduced to ashes and over one hundred of the inhabitants were captured, put in irons aboard the pirates' ships which set sail immediately for Algeria. Davis goes on to describe the terrible fate awaiting these unfortunate prisoners. He emphasises especially the horror in store for the chieftain's beautiful daughter, O'Driscoll, who was chosen for a sultan's harem, but being a fiery passionate Irish girl she had her revenge. In the midst of his love-

93

making she stabbed him to death:

*She's safe—he's dead—she stabbed him in the midst of his
   serray*
And when to die a death of fire that noble maid they bore
*She only smiled—O'Driscoll's child—she thought of
   Baltimore.*

However beautiful, sad, touching and dramatic all
this is, it is but a romantic figment of Davis's imagination
built around an entirely different set of circumstances.
What really happened is as follows: There were no Irish in
Baltimore at the time, only a colony of English settlers who
had driven the native Irish out of their houses, lands and
property. A kinsman of one of the dispossessed Irish named
John Hackett, was fishing off the Old Head of Kinsale one
June day in 1631 when he was approached by two Barbary
corsairs under the command of a Dutch captain named
Matthew Reis, who suggested that he should pilot them
into Kinsale for a good reward. Hackett, who knew immediately what they were up to, did some quick thinking. Kinsale
was too well guarded, he told them, and too dangerous to
attack, but he knew of another place, called Baltimore,
where there were plenty of strong healthy men and women
and which was completely without protection. Hackett had
seized on his chance to have revenge on the English settlers
in Baltimore, so he piloted Reis there arriving about ten
o'clock at night, and they anchored east of the Whale Rock
at the entrance to the Eastern Hole. The village at that time
was on the high ground over a gully to the east of the
Beacon road. About 2 a.m. they launched their attack,
sacked the village and took one hundred and seventeen
captives, and by the time word got to the English naval
ships in Kinsale the corsairs were gone. Some years later the
English government sent out a Mr Carson with a large sum
of money to ransom the captives but he succeeded in
buying back only a few at a figure of thirty-eight pounds
each. But none of them ever came back to Baltimore.
Very understandably they preferred to stay in their native

heath in England. John Hackett had to go on the run but he was eventually captured and hanged, and like so many others he was regarded by the English as a traitor but the native Irish saw him as a great patriot. There was of course no 'O'Driscoll's child' among the captives. The planters had long since obliterated all the O'Driscolls around Baltimore. A perusal of some of the names of the captives will show that there was not a single Irish name among them: Arnold, Broodbrooke, Chimon, Harris, Norwood, Heard, Punnery, Large, Flomer, Watts, etc.

All this however does not take away from the beauty of the poem or the greatness of Davis as a writer. Most of us see things and hear sounds, but a writer is different. He experiences everything and then communicates it. He is not concerned with accuracy but he is concerned with truth, and truth is a very relative thing. It is significant that when Pilate asked Jesus Christ: 'What is Truth?' he got no answer. Davis took an incident with all its pain and sorrow and turned it into a thing of beauty. There are two ways of representing a beautiful tree. You can take a photo of it which will give accuracy, or you can paint a portrait which will give truth. Writers and poets do not take literary photographs, they paint literary portraits. A writer takes the incidents of life, absorbs them into his mind and soul and then presents the result to the world, in much the same way as a housewife takes flour and yeast and milk, adds to them the external element of heat and turns out a bastable cake. A writer's profession is one of the hardest and loneliest professions of all. He is turned in upon himself trying to orchestrate what he thinks and feels. He has to listen to his own soul and to what it is trying to say to him and then he has to express that in the simplest and clearest of language. This has been the cause of great torment and suffering to all good writers. Frank O'Connor wrote most of his short stories over and over again before he released them. Somerset Maughan did the same. Maupassant wrote *Boule de Suiffe* more than twenty times before he published it but when he did he became famous overnight. The literary world recognised it at once as a true masterpiece. We all know Keats beautiful poem which begins with the line

A thing of beauty is a joy for ever

When Keats wrote this first it was

A thing of beauty is a constant joy

He felt instinctively that this was wrong and he tried and tried again to improve on it but failed. Then one day, more than six months later he was in a coffee house with a friend when he suddenly shouted 'I have it. I have it' and he wrote on a scrap of paper:

A thing of beauty is a joy for ever

The friend looked at what he had written and said: 'That line will live forever.'

'Creation realised at the price of a great deal of work,' said Michelangelo, 'must in spite of the truth appear easy and effortless. The great rule is to take much trouble to produce things that seem to have cost none.' And in another context Biot said, 'There is nothing so easy as what was discovered yesterday, nor so difficult as what will be discovered tomorrow.' The public of course does not know or suspect this. Indeed they think writing is effortless, and they will be the writer's most savage detractor. If they do not like what he writes they will take their revenge by ignoring him and if they do like what he writes they will still take their revenge by corrupting him if they can. That is why all great writers have cultivated an iron will, a detachment of spirit, an indifference to the curses or cheers of the crowd. Fame can destroy a man just as easily as failure. 'The most dangerous moment in life,' said Napoleon, 'is the moment of success.' If Davis had concentrated on strict historical accuracy, and on public opinion, his *Sack of Baltimore* would be as dull as ditch-water. As it is it is a superb piece of creative writing which has brought joy and pleasure to thousands of readers.

There is usually a heavy confused sea at the entrance to

the Gaiscanaun Sound, that treacherous stretch of water which separates Sherkin Island from Cape Clear. The tide was flooding and the slight North-West breeze was blowing against it so this dusted up a bit of a sea, not particularly perilous but unpleasant. Maxie, with that strange instinct which animals have for danger, removed himself from the forward deck and made his way down to the cabin where he coiled up on the floor and closed his eyes well before we hit the rough patch. It was not as unpleasant as I expected. *Dualla* plunged and bounced and tossed on the crests and in the troughs of the snarling waves, but it was all over in ten minutes and we were in smooth water again. Then Maxie opened his eyes, yawned and stretched himself and came back on deck to lie in the sun.

There is an old superstition that everyone who passes through the Gaiscanaun Sound for the first time should compose a verse in its honour to have luck for the future. When O'Donovan Rossa, the leader of the Fenians, was going through it for the first time one of the six oarsmen in the boat reminded him of the old custom. There and then Rossa composed and recited aloud a verse in the Irish language which translated says:

Oh white-breasted Gaiscanaun of the angriest current
Let me and all in this boat go past you in safety;
Stay calm and don't drown me my secret, beloved one,
And I'll give you my word that to Clear I'll never return.

Years later one of the crew of that boat emigrated to America and got employment as a fisherman on a trawler out of Boston and one day when they were fishing far out to sea a gale blew up and they had to run to New York for shelter. Weary wet and hungry they adjourned to a local tavern for refreshments. The Cape Clear man thought that the waiter who served them looked very like O'Donovan Rossa. He knew that Rossa was on his keeping from the English with a big price on his head so he did not wish to approach him in case it was not him, or in case he would give the game away. So with all the shrewdness and tact of a Caper he recited out loud the verse Rossa composed when crossing the Gaiscanaun. The waiter jumped with astonishment. It was Rossa. He threw his arms round the Caper and said:

'You must be a son of Fineen from the Island.'

'I am indeed the very man,' replied the Caper.

Whereupon Rossa gave them the best of drink and food in the house, for it was owned by Rossa himself, and they stayed three days and not a penny would he accept from them in payment.

I sailed along quite close to the rocky cliffs of Cape Clear and passed a series of points and inlets with such wonderful and unusual names that they must have been thought up first day by a race of people steeped in rhythm and music: Tonenaginkeenee, Boilgeen, Reenrourbeg, Carrigancuraun, Coolvaw, Lehanaun, Coosangaslawk, Coosanglanierig, Coosnaboilge, Deedaunmuar, and many others. Indeed every place-name in Cape has the ring of song about it. In no time at all I came to the opening between Bream Point and Bullig Point, which leads into South Harbour, and exactly three hours and fifteen minutes out from Baltimore, I brought *Dualla* to a halt and dropped anchor in one-and-a-half fathoms of water so pure and clear that I could nearly see the hook biting it. After a quick light lunch I rowed ashore with Maxie, since, like us human beings, he had a little matter to attend to, and unlike us human beings he's not a bit ashamed to attend to it in public.

It was a delightful afternoon so I went for a long stroll up over the hills, past the little schoolhouse, towards the eastern end of the island. Compared with other European islands Clear is gradually reverting to a primitive condition—untilled fields, overgrown fences, ruined cottages—but perhaps that, and the freedom to wander at will without running up against *Verboten* notices, is what gives it its peculiar charm, and makes you want to return again and again. The island is teeming with rabbits who take little notice of passers-by and in nearly every field they sat in circles looking solemnly at each other like as if they were sitting in council deliberating on problems of great weight and import affecting the destiny of their world. Indeed they paid little or no attention to Maxie either, and I was delighted to see that he did not make the slightest attempt to chase them. Here we were on a dream island, wild animals, a tame animal and a human being respecting each other's rights and all enjoying to the full the peaceful, rapturous, summer's day. I wandered leisurely along the rugged path until I came to the cross roads at Killicknaforavane and here I swung back west, past the little chapel, towards Trá Kiaran and the North Harbour. There are not enough superlatives in the English language to describe the view from this elevated road; to the east Carbery and all its three hundred isles, to the north Mount Gabriel and the Kerry mountains peeping over its shoulder, to the west the Mizen, the Bull Lighthouse, and the majestic Fastnet, and traversing everything the heaving, restless sea. I paused for a moment to absorb it all but once again, 'the beauty of this world hath made me sad'—this tragic beauty, this sad song of human limitations. Keats, who was the great poet of melancholy and mortality, is my kindred spirit. He was vividly aware of the conflict between transience and permanence, between sadness and joy, in every facet of human life. He saw so clearly what most human beings like to blot out of their minds that, 'all we have loved, or shall love, must die'. The price of all laughter and merriment is death. The almost beatific beauty of the Nightingale's song awakened in him feelings of melancholy:

> *Fade far away, dissolve and quite forget*
> *What thou amongst the leaves hast never known*
> *The weariness the fever and the fret*
> *Here, where men sit and hear each other groan*
> *Where palsy shares a few, sad, last grey hairs*
> *Where youth grows pale, and spectre-thin and dies,*
> *Where but to think is to be full of sorrow*
> *And leaden-eyed despairs*

Where Beauty cannot keep her lustrous eyes,
Or new love pine at them beyond tomorrow.

But no matter how sad and dismal things are there is always hope. 'God will wipe away all tears from their eyes,' says St John. 'There will be no more death, and no more mourning or sadness. The world of the past is gone.' A man can live without friends, without money, without health, without anything, but he cannot live without trust in a better future. Cicero said that there is nothing so beautiful, but that there is something still more beautiful, of which the present is a mere image and expression — a something which can neither be perceived by the eyes, the ears nor any of the senses; we feel it in the yearnings of our souls, and this very thought is the one which leads us straight to God and to immortality. And deep down in his soul Keats believed that too:

Thou wast not born for death, immortal Bird!
No hungry generations tread thee down,
The voice I hear this passing night was heard
In ancient days by emperor and clown:
Perhaps the self-same song that found a path
Through the sad heart of Ruth, when, sick for home
She stood in tears amid the alien corn;
The same that oft times hath
Charmed magic casements, opening on the foam
Of perilous seas and faery lands forlorn.

On my way down I dropped in for a few moments to the Irish College run by Gaedhalachas Teoranta, Colaiste Ciaran, where hundreds of children come from all parts of Ireland during the summer to learn the Irish language. This college is now recognised as one of the best in the country but for me its importance does not lie so much in that, as in the fact that the founding of this college by outsiders nearly twenty years ago was a vote of confidence in Cape Clear and its people at a time when everybody had ignored them

100

and they had hit rock bottom. This college was established by a group of Cork city people without hope of any financial reward but merely as a practical vote of confidence in one of the last living Gaeltachts in the country.

As classes were in full swing I did not go into the building but continued my way onwards towards North Harbour. As I got nearer the incline became so steep that I was glad I was going down instead of trying to climb up. Trá Kiaran, which is North Harbour, is the hub of the island. It is called after St Kiaran, the patron said of the Cape, who was born on the island one hundred years before St Patrick came to Ireland. He went abroad and forty years later came back as bishop. He seems to have been a man of formidable means, for his cow-house had ten gates, ten special stalls for ten cows, and the milk from these cows was distributed free to the islanders. So that not alone were they the first to embrace Christianity but they were the first to benefit from a free milk scheme. As well as Christianity the free milk has survived to the present day, but the Capers have improved on the latter as they now have very many more free benefits, including a free dole. Kiaran was an austere man who ate only one meal a day which consisted of a mouthful of barley and a pint of cold water. He dressed himself in deer skins and slept on a flat rock. He was in the true tradition of the old Irish saints who were noted more for their severity than for their human kindness. Isn't it extraordinary how power and influence can corrupt the simple message of Christ? The old Irish saints, in their self-righteousness lost all contact with the message of the Gospel, an example of which can be seen in the famous laws they drew up for the conduct of affairs in the early Irish Church. Here are some of them. Try not to laugh:

1. A monk and a virgin who have come from two different areas must not stay in the same inn, travel in the same chariot or speak to each other.
2. A Christian who consults a soothsayer or commits fornication shall do penance for one year.
3. He who forgets to pray before and after work shall be punished with twelve strokes.

4. He who does not control his cough during divine service shall receive six strokes.

5. If a married man commits adultery he must fast on bread and water for one year and may not live with his wife.

6. If a married man seduce a consecrated virgin he must fast on bread and water for one year and for the next two years abstain from wine and meat and at no time may he have relations with his wife.

7. If a man has relations with his slave he must sell her at once and abstain from his wife for a year.

8. If a man has a wife who is barren he must live with her in a state of chastity and all relations are forbidden.

9. Married couples must abstain from sexual relations for three periods of forty days each year, to be agreed between them. Neither shall they have relations on Saturday or Sunday nights.

10. If a layman has intercourse with an unmarried woman, that is, a widow or a virgin, he shall do penance for a year if she is a widow and for two years if she is a virgin.

11. If a layman commits perjury he must sell all his property, give the money to the poor and enter a monastery.

12. The man who desires to commit fornication but is prevented, shall do penance for a year.

13. After the birth of a child married couples shall refrain from relations for thirty-three days in the case of a son and for sixty-six days in the case of a daughter.

Then there was a whole set of definitions so that nobody could claim ignorance.

A Special Penance: One hundred psalms and one hundred genuflections daily, or three days in the tomb of a dead saint, without food, drink or sleep, or twelve days and nights with no food, or forty days on bread and water, or forty psalms and sixty genuflections every three hours.

There were hundreds more. If they were in vogue now I know a lot of my friends who would have no weight problems. Sensibly enough, however, the Pope at two Councils in 813 and 829 formally condemned them as grossly unchristian, but he had to threaten to excommunicate the whole Irish hierarchy before they gave them up. In his delightful paperback *Sex and Marriage in Ancient Ireland* Dr Patrick C. Power shows how liberal and humane the old Irish Brehon laws were in regard to sexual lapses and how much nearer they were to the spirit of Christ than the ecclesiastical laws which replaced them.

Kiaran built a small church overlooking the harbour and although the buildings one sees today date only from the twelfth century they were undoubtedly built on the site of St Kiaran's original church. The graveyard surrounding the church is still in use and I searched through the growth until I found what I was looking for—the grave of Conor Mac Eirevaun, who was nearly nine feet tall and was a man of immense proportions and legendary strength. The Capers tell a story about him which shows that the abuse of trade unionism didn't begin yesterday. He was standing one day on the quays of Cork City and he saw six men hauling on a heavy chain without any success. When he asked what they were doing they told him that they were trying to raise a ships anchor weighing more than six hundredweight and they were only able to budge it a few inches every day. Conor caught the end of the chain and the first jerk he gave he loosened it, the second jerk he brought it to the bottom of the wall and the third jerk he landed it out on the quay. Instead of thanks all he got from the men was abuse. 'You have done the six of us out of a week's work,' they shouted angrily. 'We'll report you to the union.' When Conor heard this he caught up the anchor and threw it out twice as far as it had been.

'There now,' he said as he left them. 'Go and earn your hire!'

The little graveyard is now quite clean but I remember some years ago I found it almost impossible to pick my steps through the ancient ruins because the entire place was littered with excrement of long-haired beardies and their weirdies who had set several tents in the shelter of the graveyard walls and who lay in the nearby field with their bellies upturned to the sun like dead wasps in autumn. It is to the eternal credit of the Capers that some time afterwards they descended in force on these receptacles of dirt, flung them, together with their tents, into the harbour at low water so that they wouldn't be drowned, but would get a good washing, and they have never returned to the island since.

Not far from the ruined church is possibly one of the oldest Christian relics in Ireland. It is a large boulder about four feet high and two feet across upon which are carved two crosses said to have been cut out by Kiaran himself, and embedded by him in the hillside so that the Capers would never forget him.

As I was retracing my steps across the harbour I heard a loud yell and Maxie came running towards me whimpering. He was followed by two young men with sticks in their hands who stopped when they saw me.

'Is that your dog,' they called out to me.

I knew then Maxie was in trouble.

'No,' I lied. 'He belongs to the parish priest.'

They paused for a moment and then went away. I found out later that they were from the Bird Watching Centre on the other side of the pier. Some rare birds had been reported in the area and the watchers had placed choice pieces of liver and meat in several likely spots to attract the birds. But Maxie got there first and was finishing off the last piece of liver when he was surprised with a kick in the behind from one of the angry watchers, who could hardly be blamed, seeing that their hard and carefully planned work had gone for nothing.

I strolled back to South Harbour, but instead of going aboard *Dualla* and cooking a meal I went into a delightful little restaurant called *Tír-na-nÓg* and stood myself a treat. I had a large juicy steak, home-made bread and a pot of strong tea, served by a beautiful girl named Mairead, who gave Maxie a plate of bones right under my table. No 'dogs not wanted' here.

Later that night I went to a pub. It was crowded but nevertheless Maxie found a spot under my stool, where, indifferent to all, he went to sleep. There was a gay singsong in full swing but most of the songs were in English which is a sign of the changing times in Cape Clear. I could not help noticing a handsome young man who sang very beautifully and it was only later I saw he was blind and accompanied by a guide-dog. His face, obviously moulded by contemplation rather than competition, was one of the happiest I had ever seen. This carefree cheerful atmosphere was marred, but for a moment only, by the appearance of two wealthy yachtsmen with the mean bitter faces of men who started out in life seeking material success only, and who found it. Every community, including the yachting, has a few of these sad empty creatures who must do the 'in thing', which is to dress up in the evening in a navy-blue reefer jacket with club buttons, dark flannels, white shirt, multi-coloured scarf and a peaked cap not unlike that worn by a chucker-out at a Soho night-club. They must then proceed to all the pubs of character in whatever harbour they may be in, elbow their way up to the counter, shake hands with the owner and call him by his first name as if they were old friends, have one drink and then move off. Any idea that they might enjoy a bit of companionship or a song would be completely alien to them. They never enjoy anything in their lives with the possible exception of their daily excursion to the lavatory. When you translate all this nonsense into plain English what they are really saying is: 'Inside I am empty. I must act like this in order to impress you and try to prove that I am better than you are. Please pity me, and help me by reacting as if I were real.' The two who came in were of that ilk, and everyone including the owner breathed a sigh of relief when they left for the next pub and the same ritual. Mind you, while they called the owner by his first name they expected to be addressed as 'sir' in return. The late Sonny Sullivan of Crookhaven was once asked why he called these parasites 'sir'. His answer was brilliant.

'I call them "sir" because 'tis good for business — but I spell it "C-U-R".'

There was an old Islander sitting beside me and we had a long chat in Irish. It was wonderful to speak the language again and to hear the rich melodious words coming with such fluency and ease from his lips. As the night went on and we spoke together I felt as if I were bridging the centuries, reaching back into the past, immersing myself in a culture that was still old when Moses was a boy. The old man's story was a sad one: 'The great days of the island are drawing to a close,' he lamented. 'The islanders are no longer the proud independent people they used to be. Instead of working all they have in their heads now is how to get what they can for nothing. When I was a boy we worked twelve hours a day. We took off our coats, and sometimes our shirts too, if we had one, and dug, and ploughed and harrowed and grew our own crops to feed man and beast; we ground our own corn to make bread, we raised pigs, cows and goats so that we had little to buy from the mainland except a grain of tea, a bit of sugar and a handful of tobacco. I remember when there was thirty boats fishing from North Harbour, and the money we got for the fish paid for the extras. But today we have bottled gas, electricity, white bakers bread, vegetables in tins — everything brought in on the mail boat. The fields and gardens of the island are growing wild, overrun by furze bushes and you'd hardly hear the crowing of a cock or the lowing of a cow from one end of the island to the other. And that's all because we want everything for nothing, free milk, free turf, free dung, free food and worst of all free dole. The men of the island can stay in bed now until dinner-time and need never do a day's work. There's hardly any children on the island now but in my day every man had a big family and enough sons to carry his coffin to the graveyard and bury him dacent. Many's the man had fourteen or fifteen children and no neighbour had to help him to blow the bellows either. All the joy and fun is now gone, and most of the people look at one another with sour faces in case one's getting more for nothing than the other. The only hope left is for some smart man to take charge of the country, stop making idlers out of us and make us work for our money. We might not have as much that way but we could hold up our heads high and not be ashamed of ourselves as a people. Anyway I shouldn't be annoying you with all this ould guff. We'll have another drink.' He was a proud man and he insisted on standing to me. The crowd now began a kind of a community sing-song in Irish, in which the old man joined, and time slipped quietly and pleasantly by until closing time.

In the dark, Maxie and myself made our way unsteadily back to South Harbour and to *Dualla*, and there soothed by the gentle music of the lapping water in the glorious silence of the night, I fell asleep.

7

In the morning I was awakened as usual by Maxie rubbing his furry head and cold nose across my face. I dressed and brought him ashore so that he might attend to his simple needs with the serene unconcern of innocence. He was in no hurry, and with admirable good taste he examined several potential locations finally choosing one where the green grass of the island met the grey rock of the sea, giving him the best of both worlds. We went for a short brisk appetising walk to the North Harbour and I made quite sure that he did not go within the bawl of an ass of the Bird Watching house. Being the alleged property of the parish priest would hardly save him a second time. When I got back to *Dualla* I shaved off a strong beard while the breakfast was cooking and made myself look a little less like

Robinson Crusoe and more like a member of the Royal Cork Yacht Club, the oldest yacht club in the world. While I was enjoying breakfast out on deck I had a rather intriguing experience. On the island, somewhat west of where *Dualla* was anchored, there is a very well-kept and roomy Youth Hostel, which in the past was a Rectory and which is now used mainly by young hikers, mostly in their late teens or early twenties. They generally arrive in couples and stay for a few days but for those in the first flush of love there is one big stumbling block. There are two large dormitories and the males are strictly separated from the females so that the Romeos and Juliets find this something of an unreasonable strain. To overcome such a serious drawback to a gay holiday they stroll after breakfast, by way of no harm, up the side of a heather-covered mountain sloping down to the sea, east of the hostel. When they believe they are well out of sight of roads and houses they get down to the task of expressing their Christian devotion for one another. So on this lovely summer's morning I saw four or five young couples hastily moving into position on different parts of the mountain which rose straight out of the sea directly in front of *Dualla*. Now they made one rather serious miscalculation. It did not seem to dawn on them that they were visible from the sea, so sitting unobtrusively in the cockpit of *Dualla* I had a Dress-Circle view of a most realistic Irish version of *Oh! Calcutta*, and judging from the various acrobatics and gymnastics I saw it occurred to me what a great pity D. H. Lawrence had not spent some of his youth on this holy island of St Kiaran. If he had, then *Lady Chatterley's Lover* might have been a much more enjoyable, humorous and less depressing book. I think it was the great Catholic writer Hilaire Belloc who said that if sex can make you laugh everything is alright but if it does not make you laugh there are dark problems on the horizon; so when I stopped laughing and began to feel nostalgic for the long lost days of my youth, I thought it was time to be shortening the journey before me, so I upped sail, broke out the anchor and headed for the open sea, hoping that the clear fresh pure air of the Atlantic would put more wholesome thoughts into my head. 'He who fights and runs away will live to fight another day.' I envied Maxie who was in no way affected as he lay asleep in the cockpit, which again proves the superiority of animals over human beings.

The cliffs on either side of South Harbour are high and rugged and the continual lashing of wild seas have sculptured out innumerable caves on either side where an incredible variety of sea birds make their home. It was another beautiful day. The wind was gently blowing from the North-West but very shortly after I cleared Bream Point, heading towards the Bill of Cape Clear, I suddenly ran into a nasty tidal race caused by the ebb tide flowing against the wind which sent *Dualla* plunging and pitching from one confused mass of water to another. Luckily it did not last more than twenty minutes and I was in clear water again but if the wind had been a point or two stronger it would have been thoroughly nasty and perhaps even dangerous. I set *Dualla* on a course leaving the Western Calf to starboard, past the Amelia buoy, through the channel separating Long Island from Castle Island, and thence into the safety and tranquil shelter of Schull harbour. I set the self-steering and sat out on deck gazing back at the haven of peace and beauty I had just left. I had never before seen Cape Clear looking so magnificent. The whole island seemed to be carpeted in purple heather dotted here and there with quaint white-washed cottages, through which little winding pathways climbed onwards and upwards into the warm rising sun. I thought of the words of that gifted Irish poet William A. Byrne:

> *The purple heather is the cloak*
> *God gave the moorland brown*
> *But man has made a pall of smoke*
> *To lay about the town.*

And I thought too of that curious race of people who inhabited Cape Clear island and who are so very different from those living on the mainland, and of the sad story told me the evening before by the old man. For as far back as we can go with any reasonable certainty the Capers were a distinct community and kept themselves separate by inter-marrying with their own, which must surely make them the very purest of Celts. Until about 1750 they had their own king, usually an O'Driscoll, and their own code of laws and although I have searched high up and low down I have failed to come across this code. All I can find out is that it was an oral code handed down from father to son and very strictly administered. Punishment was generally a fine but for a serious offence it was banishment from the island. Because the climate is particularly healthy, there is little serious disease and people usually lived to a very great age. They had a reputation for shrewdness and worldly wisdom so that an enterprising shopkeeper in Skibbereen once put a notice in his window: SHOP HERE AND BE AS CLEVER AS A CAPER. To go along with this great cleverness they were renowned for their diplomacy—they would never offend a potential money-spender no matter how hard they were provoked. There is a story told of a Caper who was doing gillie, on a day's shooting, to a titled lady of gentle birth. She must have been somewhat of a vulgar creature in so far as she kept breaking wind regularly much to the discomfort of the Caper who was down-wind from her all the time and who patiently suffered the unpleasant consequences. From under a clump of sedge she sprung a snipe and quickly raised the gun to fire. Something went wrong however and instead of firing the gun she broke wind again, this time with a thunderous report discharged straight into the Caper's face. On the principle that the customer is always right the Caper shouted 'Quick, my lady! Fire the second barrel while the bird is still in the air.'

I was once told another story of a Caper who was caught out in a bad storm at sea, so bad indeed that it could easily have fatal consequences. Anxious to keep both God and the devil on his hands in case anything happened he prayed aloud: 'Oh God, if there be a God, save my soul, if I have one.'

During the Famine the proselytisers came to Cape and handed out soup to those who turned Protestant. The Capers, being all things to all men, took the soup, read the bible, but when the Famine was over, went back to their old faith. Once during that time a hot-gospeller assembled all the male population in the church and gave them a fiery sermon on the evils of drink. He had a glass of water and a glass of alcohol on the table with him. He dropped a live worm into the glass of water, and the worm just swam gaily around. He dropped a second live worm into the glass of alcohol and it immediately shrivelled up and died.

'Now what important lesson does that example teach us?' he bellowed. After a short silence, one Caper bolder than the rest, spoke up from the back of the church. 'It teaches us, your reverence, that if you drink alcohol you'll never get worms.'

But despite what the old man told me Cape Clear is not dying. A new spirit of work and cooperation is pervading the island. Despite the dishonesty of successive native governments which has almost plundered the island of its more precious possession, the Irish language, more surely than the bayonets of the Black-and-Tans could ever do, the people are determined to hold on to it. The politicians who in the past strangled their spirit by that diabolical vote-catching weapon, the dole, may have a second think coming to them. A race with a great heritage is not easily destroyed.

When I rounded the Western Calf, instead of making straight for Schull I gave way to an impulse and set course for the Carthy Islands, a dangerous cluster of rocky islets which present a frightening appearance in wild weather but which looked today like a fairy palace in *Tír-na-nÓg*. According to *The Annals of the Four Masters* Ireland was struck by some form of earthquake about the year 830 AD and this earthquake separated Long Island, Castle Island, the Carthys and perhaps even Cape Clear itself from the mainland. All the islands around here present a picture of being forcibly wrenched away against their will. The Carthys form a large circle of crags with a narrow entrance to the south and a fairy-like lagoon of magical charm and delicate beauty inside.

I dropped anchor in the spring-clear water almost at the centre and surveyed this little paradise. It was strangely still and quiet, yet not oppressive, for silence is not a dead but a very living thing. This secluded spot shows the strange wilfulness of nature which lavishes beauty where none save the adventurous few, can see it. The jagged rocks rose up in wild uneven meaningless forms like the pieces of sculpture at a Rosc exhibition, and had that sense of eeriness about them that I would not have been surprised if a dinosaur moved out to greet me, but the only living things were the birds and the seals singing duets to each other—duets of annoyance because their peace was disturbed.

After lunch, I stayed there more than an hour, my thoughts stretched out across the sea like an uneven silver path to the horizon, one stream coming after the other, each more meaningless than the last. Had I written them down as they came the result would be at least as boring as James Joyce. But no thoughts however stupid could take from the beauty of this little bit of heaven. I listened to the gentle sound of the waves that have nothing to do but make music all day long. I felt the soft Northern wind fingering through my hair like the gentle caress of a woman in love:

> *O world invisible, we view thee,*
> *O world intangible, we touch thee,*
> *O world unknowable, we know thee,*
> *Inapprehensible, we clutch thee.*

This is a delightful lagoon that should not be missed by any yachtsman no matter what hurry is on him.

The run up to Schull is a short one. I left the Amelia buoy to starboard, slipped past Copper Point with its towering white beacon, sailed in between Schull Point on the west and Cosheen Point on the east. Making sure not to go too near the red perch which marks the Bull rock, and just east of the pier in two fathoms of water, I dropped anchor as the evening sun was beginning to throw its rose light on the calm still waters of the bay.

After dinner I rowed Maxie ashore to pay his respects to Schull and we then went for a stroll together through the quiet streets of this pleasant village which has very largely retained its character and old-worldliness. Newcomers have built their bungalows on the outskirts along the shore and most of these bungalows are tasteful and pleasant to look at. Like Baltimore, Schull has a great advantage in having no sandy beaches. These beaches seem to attract caravans, tents, broken-down coaches and a host of other temporary dwellings which bring about a terrible litter and sanitation problem and a real hazard to health. Unlike continental countries we have not yet got around to controlling these matters. Schull is a clean well-kept town of charm and individuality. I love to stroll around the streets of little towns admiring and criticising the design of the houses and shops, the varied colour schemes, the unusual surnames, but above all, the strange notices one sees from time to time in different windows. Every little town has its own peculiarities. One year during a prolonged spell of drought in Baltimore there was a notice in a lavatory: *Owing to shortage of water pull chain for big job only.* In Skibbereen an enterprising grocer had this notice in his window: *Our tea is blended to suit your water.* In Castletownbere there was a notice in the window of a private house: *For sale – two single beds and carpet. Carpet slightly worn.* From Castletownsend: *For sale – Georgian table almost new.* In a supermarket: *We lose 10p on every sale but we make it up because of our enormous turnover.* Perhaps the classic of all was the notice once nailed to the W.C. in the Bird Watching house on Cape Clear: *Gentlemen. If possible use the bushes at the east end of the house. Not the Elsan. Thank you.* For some years I have been collecting these notices and I have now close on one hundred, but one of my great sorrows is the loss of a magnificent collection of Thanksgiving notices, mostly from Irish provincial newspapers which I spent almost twenty years putting together. I left it after me in a hotel room and it has not turned up since. There were two real

113

gems in this collection. The first from a religious paper: *Grateful thanks to the most Sacred Heart of Jesus for the victory of Cork over Kerry in the Munster Final. Although I could not attend the match I listened in on the radio and every time the referee blew his whistle I said 'Sacred Heart of Jesus I place my trust in thee.'* The second was from a provincial paper: *Grateful thanks to the Sacred Heart of Jesus for my obtaining the Old Age Pension five years before it was due.*

But this evening I only found two notices in Schull. One in the window of a guest house said: *Bed and Breakfast. No Hippies.* The other in the window of a pub said simply: *No Tinkers.* So I strolled further along towards the end of the village and walked out the Colla road until I came to what is possibly the most picturesque spot in all Schull, overlooking the harbour and within sound of the sea – the graveyard. Graveyards have always pulled me like a magnet and I hardly ever miss an opportunity of visiting one if I have any bit of time to spare. In a graveyard I always meet up with the great reality that I must die and there are very few thoughts more sobering than that one. The end price of the 'eat drink and be merry' is the silence of the grave. All around me were the remains of those who lived as we live now, whose pulses beat, whose breath flowed freely, whose blood ran joyously through the veins, who laughed and cried, who loved and hated, who sailed their boats, and besported themselves on the green fields, who became successes or dejected failures. They are all together now and there is nothing more life can do to them. The very headstones seem to cry out *Hodie mihi! Cras tibi! Today for me; tomorrow for you!*

> *Observe the dew-drenched rose of Tyrian grain –*
> *A rose today. But will you ask in vain*
> *Tomorrow what it is; and yesterday*
> *It was the dust, the sunshine, and the rain.*

If the certainty of death with all its ghastly skulls and

bones and rotting coffins is such a reality how can we ever enjoy life? How can we love and laugh and sing and dance if we know for certain that soon we will be buried, to rot and decay and be forgotten, that everything we achieve is but a 'snowflake on the desert's dusty face'. If death were only a probability one could understand the lust for life, but death is as certain as night and day. How then can we be so joyful and sometimes so happy when this terrible savage fate awaits us? I believe it is because we know in the very depths of our being that we are immortal, that we never really die. If Keats could say of the nightingale:

Thou wast not born for death immortal bird

surely we can say, looking into the upturned innocent face of a child:

Thou wast not born for death immortal one.

It is with this moment of realisation that a graveyard takes on a different aspect. It is no longer a place of gloom or sorrow or sadness, but almost a place of envy, where all suffering ends and eternal youth begins. The dead are free from the pains and sufferings of this life. They exist in one complete act of perpetual love. Their intellects are so powerful that they see all the mysteries of life in one vision. They know the answers to each question that ever baffled the human mind. They know the last revealing chapter in the mysterious book of life. They are so far superior to us in beauty, love and happiness as to defy understanding by an imperfect human brain. It is they who must surely pity us. But a graveyard should serve as a warning too. A warning that beyond the grave there are no kings or queens, lords or dukes, no decorations or medals and above all no money. The dead face their new world holding in their hands only what they *were* in this life, not what they *had*, only their unselfishness, their generosity, their sacrifices and their love. All other possessions must be left behind to contribute to the unhappiness and misery of those who inherit them.

The Moving Finger writes: and, having writ,
Moves on: nor all thy piety nor wit
Shall lure it back to cancel half a line,
Nor all thy tears wash out a word of it.

I strolled in and out through the lines of graves with all these thoughts tumbling through my mind. The red glow of the setting sun had transformed the sea into a vast floor of glittering copper. Twilight was beginning to brood over the harbour as the clouds slowly folded themselves into night. A mood of deep sorrow mingled with exhilarating hope possessed my soul as I rambled back towards the village. I paused before the pub with the *No Tinkers* sign in the window. Loud sounds of laughter, singing and jollification wafted towards the street. My mood changed and I went in. I had forgotten the lessons of the graveyard.

The pub was crowded, and I was surprised to find, sitting in one corner, a tinker with his wife, whom I knew of old. He was one of the wealthy tinkers earning twenty or thirty thousand pounds a year, tax free, rates free, rent free. He was clean, well-dressed in a grey tweed suit, new shirt and red tie, while the wife was bedecked with multi-coloured rings, necklaces and ribbons and looked for all the world like a committee boat on a regatta day. As far as I remembered neither of them could read or write so the notice in the window meant little to them, and indeed the landlord was unlikely to suspect that two such well dressed customers could be tinkers. They were strangers to Schull, they told me; this was their first time there. As we lowered our pints they confided to me that they were clapping the south coast. Let me explain. This particular kind of tinker earns substantial money from calling uninvited on isolated houses and buying furniture, silver, paintings or any form of antique they can lay their hands on. In Ireland they are known as 'clappers'. In England they are called 'higglers'. They live mostly in luxury caravans, have no fixed abode, and work the country high up and low down as the exigencies of business demand. It is variously estimated that they send at least

116

one million pounds worth of antiques out of the country in any one year. Although virtually uneducated many of them are extremely cunning, and they tend to follow the line of the rivers because in these fertile valleys the best houses are located. Their techniques vary but generally combine a mixture of charm and threat. When a door is opened to them they burst straight into the hall usually brandishing wads of notes, all calculated to terrify and mesmerise the unfortunate housewife. They tell her they are buying old unwanted furniture suitable for sets in R.T.E., although they are cute enough not to say that they work for R.T.E., and that they pay the very highest prices. Then one of them opens the sitting-room door, looks quickly around and offers perhaps one hundred pounds for a framed Papal Blessing or a treasured wedding photo. The great skill here is to offer high money for something of spiritual or sentimental value which is more than likely not for sale at any price. This manoeuvre implants in the mind of the bewildered housewife that they are big generous spenders, and the earlier mention of R.T.E. suggests that they can afford to be so. In the meantime they will have spotted a piece of furniture, or old silver or painting, and when the woman explains that the Papal Blessing or wedding photograph is not for sale they then plead with her not to let them go away empty handed—they are very poor and have wives and children to support etc. etc. So please. . . The woman in her kindness hesitates and at this moment twenty pounds in notes is pushed into her hand, and before she knows what has happened they have removed the antique previously spotted. She is usually too frightened and at the same time too full of pity to object. After all they must be giving her more than a fair price—didn't they offer one hundred pounds for a photo that costs only a few shillings? And so for the twenty pounds they get something worth several hundred or indeed several thousand pounds. Another special trick they have when they see a chair, chest of drawers, table, clock or other valuable antique is to say that the nuns in a nearby convent have the

117

comrade of it and have asked them to look out for one the same so as to complete the pair.

Their techniques usually follow a pattern. 1. Subtle intimidation. 2. Creating the idea that they are big spenders. 3. Producing large wads of notes. 4. Arousing a certain amount of pity, and 5. Returning again and again pestering people until they finally sell to get rid of them. In this way Irish housewives have parted with virtually millions of pounds worth of antiques for a song.

While we were enjoying our pints in the gay atmosphere of the pub he told me of some recent 'kills' he had. A pair of candlesticks for six pounds sold for one thousand five hundred pounds; a French table for two hundred pounds sold for three thousand five hundred; a Victoria Cross for five pounds sold for two thousand five hundred; a Dresden figure for one pound sold for three hundred and fifty.

'Since you are hardly able to read or write,' I interrupted, 'how do you know the value of things?'

'Ah, I'm not that bad,' he said. 'I can read figures fairly well. I go to every auction where there's antiques, and I spend a day examining all the items. Then the day of the auction I listen to the prices and they stay in my head forever. As well as that I go through everything in every antique shop in the country when I'm passing, and again I learn the prices off by heart. I never forget a price. After a year of that kind of going-on I'm ready for anything. No one will fool me and I'm able to fool the fools all the time. I heard tell of a fellow that lived west of Galway, out there somewhere in Connemara, I think he was some class of show-man; well that fellow said that there's a fool born every minute and most of them live. He's me man. He was dead right. Only that most of the people are fools I'd be in the poor house long ago.'

'Do you every pay Income Tax or Turnover Tax?' I asked.

'In the name of Jaysus is it coddin' me you are. 'Tis only the fools who pay tax. I never paid it in me life and please God never will. Surely you don't expect me to pay money

118

to keep idlers and bums on the dole?'

'But how do you cover-up? How do you get away with it?' I asked.

'Now you must take me for one of them fools that the Connemara man was talking about,' he answered. 'How do I know that you haven't a cousin or near relation with them tax sharks and that you wouldn't split on me. I haven't a bloody notion of telling you.'

'Anyway,' he continued, 'I have to give big money sometimes for good stuff. Now this morning I bought a picture from a respectable woman and I had to put one thousand in notes in the heel of her fist to get it. That's as true as God is over me.'

His cunning was now coming to the surface. He knew I collected old paintings and he had established a figure which he felt should be a starting point. Of course I didn't believe a word he said. More than likely he paid forty or fifty pounds for it.

'What kind of picture is it?' I asked pretending to fall into the trap.

''Tis a valuable picture,' he answered. 'With cows and goats and dogs and people and houses.'

'I suppose I'd better have a look at it,' I said finishing my drink.

'Fair enough,' he said sinking his pint. 'We'll go out to the caravan—but remember this is no cheap picture. I gave a lot of money for it.'

We left the pub, himself, his wife and Maxie who had been sleeping quietly under the table despite all the din. The caravan was parked about a mile outside the town, and when we got inside and lit the lights he showed me the painting. It was Dutch on panel late seventeenth century or early eighteenth century, by no means from the hand of a master, but a good amateur effort worth a few hundred pounds. I started off by offering him ten pounds.

'In the name of God,' he said turning to his wife, 'put on the kettle and make a sup of tay and let this man go home so that we can say the Rosary and go to bed. He must

119

think the two of us was born under a head of cabbage like the black snails.' We talked about other topics for a while and then came back to the picture. As a great favour he would let me have it for one thousand two hundred and fifty pounds and this was only giving him a very small profit. I then upped my bid to twenty pounds. He opened his mouth to say something then started coughing and two of his false teeth fell out. As soon as he recovered the argument started again. It went on and on for more than an hour, right through the mugs of hot tea and toast his wife gave us—not forgetting the bones of a pigs-head for Maxie. Bit by bit I had upped my bid until it now stood at one hundred pounds and he was down to seven hundred and fifty, taking a loss on the picture because, as he said, he knew my wife God rest her, a decent woman who often done him a good turn and who would surely like to have the picture in the house if she were alive. I finally stood up to leave.

'My last word is one hundred and ten pounds,' I said, 'and if you don't take that you can stuff your bloody picture you-know-where.'

'Now, now,' he said. 'Don't be so contrary. I'll tell you what I'll do. Because I wasn't able to go to your poor wife's funeral, and for ould times sake, give me one hundred and twenty five and I'll give you five pounds luck money back.'

I hesitated pretending to be unsure, but at the same time terrified lest he change his mind.

'Alright,' I said and wrote him a cheque for a hundred and twenty-five pounds.

'You'll never be sorry for this,' he said handing me a fiver having spat on it. 'And may you make a million. I took a heavy loss in honour of your wife.' He drove me back to the pier at Schull with my newly acquired picture, and a bag of crubeens for Maxie.

When I got out of the car I went around to his window.

'Tell me honestly, before you say the Rosary,' I said, 'how much did you really pay for it?'

He paused before answering and then started to laugh.

'I gave a farmer's wife twenty pounds for it this morning and she was so delighted that she promised to say a novena of rosaries for me. She wanted a few quid on the quiet that himself wouldn't know about and she made a nine-day novena to St Jude who sent me along. She said I was the dacentest man she ever met.' He paused with a merry twinkle in his eye.

'Anyway,' he said, 'may you have luck with it. Good night.'

He drove off to his Rosary and I rowed out to *Dualla* with my picture and with Maxie and his bag of crubeens.

8

Shortly after eight o'clock in the morning Maxie's furry head woke me, and I got up, rowed him ashore and went for a short walk in the fresh clear morning air before returning to *Dualla* for breakfast. There was no hurry on me, and I sat lazily in the cockpit with a mug of hot tea, just watching the activity in the harbour; lobstermen getting their pots and bait ready, trawlermen with their Aran berets mending the nets, tourists going out in small boats for a picnic or a day's fishing, little children from the cities, with their pale ashen faces, simply throwing stones in the water, thrilled with the joy of freedom. I sat there for more than two hours, just watching life pass by, with no deep profound thoughts, merely rambling along *ar bhóthairín na smaointe*, day dreaming, musing, idly letting my flights of fancy dance and frolic like fairies in a field of buttercups. Coming up to midday I managed to rouse myself sufficiently to get ready for the next and last lap of my journey, to the sheltered and picturesque harbour of Crookhaven.

It was a soft summer's day with a light South-Westerly wind which brought with it an occasional shower of gentle rain that made land and sea sparkle like a panorama of priceless gems. With only the main sail set I motored up Long Island sound past the attractive houses on the mainland tastefully perched between the red and green hedges of fuscia that meander dreamily down to the shore. This wild beauty contrasts strangely with the bare desolate landscape of Long Island itself, which is just across the sound. Although Long Island contains only one hundred and fifty-four acres of land it once supported a thriving community of two hundred and forty people. There is many a farmer in Ireland today who would complain that he cannot rear even one family on that amount of land. The islanders cultivated every arable inch and supplemented their meagre income by fishing and a little pilotage. But this world-without-dole, the world where people worked to live, is past and gone. The decay started with the Famine, followed by the sheer brutality of landlordism, and later the neglect of native governments reduced the population to a few families. There is an account in one of the earlier issues of the *Cork Examiner* of a family of eight in Long Island who had to cross to Schull at the beginning of winter and sell their boots and shoes to the highest bidder in order to pay the rent to a London landlord. They succeeded in doing so and returned to the island barefooted and remained without footwear until spring brought a few rabbits with which they made slippers from the skins. Today Long Island is inhabited mostly by visitors, who spend the summer there and lock up for the winter. Many city folk with a romantic turn of mind thought it would be heaven on earth to settle down and live on Long Island, away from it all etc., but those who tried it found out that when the winter storms and gales lashed its shores and swept over its shelterless surface, it was much more earth than heaven. Others, with a little more depth and wisdom, found out that the kingdom of peace and happiness is within everyman's soul and nowhere else and one does not need to live on an island to find it.

One of the last inhabitants of Long Island, and old man who died some years ago, had the reputation of being an expert weather forecaster. It is said that he was the seventh son of a seventh daughter and had extra-sensory powers which enabled him to see into the future. At hay-making time and harvest time farmers came from far and wide to Colla pier and crossed to the island to get his opinion on the weather. He charged a modest fee and everyone went away satisfied since his forecasts proved accurate ninety-nine percent of the time. Then one day, at harvest time, a farmer from the Beara peninsula made the long journey across the mountains to find out what the weather was going to make over the next few days as he wanted to hire some men to cut his corn. When he got to the island the old man was full of apologies because he was unable to help him.

'I'm sure right sorry,' he explained. 'You see, me bloody wireless broke down yesterday.'

Almost at the head of the sound I passed that delightful little Coney Island (did it, or the one in Baltimore or the one in New York come first?). This is as safe and sheltered an anchorage as can be found in the whole area and I once rode out a bad Westerly gale, which at times reached force ten, in the lea of this island with scarcely a ripple on the water. Croagh Bay, on the other side of the island is also an excellent anchorage, but one must be careful not to go too far in as it shelves steeply and suddenly. This bay was the main landing place for contraband goods imported by the smugglers all during the eighteenth century when this lucrative business reached astronomical proportions. The great successful smuggler of the era was the Dutchman Claus Campeon who owned a fleet of more that a hundred ships and was a millionaire several times over. Campeon, who had a faultless understanding of all politicians, kept on good terms with Lord Falkland, the King's Deputy in Ireland, and with Sir William Hull the representative of the British government in West Cork. He paid each of them a handsome percentage on all goods smuggled so that not only did they turn a blind eye to what was going on but they tipped Campeon off when any naval ships, with the task of apprehending smugglers, were in the area. All made a handsome profit so God save our Great and Glorious King.

Instead of sailing out through Goat Island Sound or Man of War Sound I continued straight on through Lough Buidhe with the half-notion in my mind that I might slip over to Goleen for an hour or two. This is a very tricky passage dotted with submerged rocks and one is well advised to keep a close eye on the chart. Once I came through an even more difficult passage between Hare Island, the Skeames and the mainland, with Mike Donoghue as a pilot. I was more than apprehensive as he grazed by rocks on all sides and at one point I asked him if he were quite sure he knew where all the rocks were. 'I'm not sure I knows where the rocks is,' he answered, 'but I bloody-well knows where they isn't.' And so with these words of wisdom in my mind I studied the chart carefully for where 'the rocks isn't' and gradually slipped out through the Barrell Sound between Duharrig islets and the mainland, passing the ruin of Leam-con Castle where in the good old days when the O'Mahonys lived there the festivities after a wedding went on for three weeks despite several attempts by the harassed owner to send the guests home. Finally in desperation the poor man had to burn down his castle to get rid of them.

As I emerged from the sound a light shower of soft summer rain began to fall and the whole of Toormore Bay was lit up by a multi-coloured rainbow turning the entire scene into a vista of enchanting beauty. Impulsively I set the self-steering and stripped naked under the gently falling rain. I felt a wonderful sensation of well-being as I rubbed the mild pearly raindrops into my parched body. In that moment it was marvellous to be alive. Just then a small rowing boat with two young girls and a man emerged from behind Castle Point. I stood up on deck and waved joyous-ly at them wishing that they too could share in this flash of exquisite beauty. Instead of waving back the girls turned their faces away and covered their heads with scarves while the man shook his fist menacingly at me. It was only then I realised I was stark naked. I quickly came to my senses, jumped into my jeans and waved again. The response was negative. The man was still shaking his fist at me as they moved away into Toormore Bay. It was then I began to panic. If they decided to go to the police I would have a squad car waiting for me at Crookhaven. My imagination began to run wild. I could visualise the newspaper headlines: LONE YACHTSMAN EXPOSES HIMSELF INDECENTLY. I could hear the charge being read out in court in the cold unemotional words of the law: '. . . in that he did on such-and-such a day, contrary to section so-and-so of the Public Morality Act of 1865 expose himself carnally to the afore-mentioned ladies and display in an obscene manner such object or objects as which they had no desire to see. . . ' I had only one line of escape and that was to pretend that I was not going to Crookhaven at all but, instead, that I was making off for France, England or some other foreign country. So I quickly changed course, put up the foresail, turned off the engine and headed *Dualla* out to sea on a course that would bring me past the Fastnet Lighthouse. and in the direction of the Scilly Islands. In this way there was a good chance they would think I was some promiscu-ous Frenchman in a hurry to get home to the fleshpots of Paris, and not used to the Christian modesty of West Cork. I knew that when I got to the Fastnet it would be safe because I would be too far out for them to see me or to distinguish *Dualla* from the many other sailing boats that are always in that area. I could then change course at my ease for Crookhaven. It meant a long extra haul, two sides of a triangle, but it would be preferable than to have to face charges in the Ballydehob District Court. As I sailed out I threw the odd furtive glance back to see what was happen-ing, and after a while I noticed that they had stopped and were no longer heading towards the shore. Through the field glasses I could see that they had begun to fish with hand-lines so it seemed as if my plan was working. I do not know who they were but if their eyes ever catch these words I would like to offer my most profuse apologies. I really did not think of what I was doing and I meant no harm. I sincerely hope that what the young ladies saw that lovely summer's day will not have any inhibiting influence on the future of their conjugal happiness.

Dualla was now dancing along the waves under full sail in a South-Westerly wind heading towards the stately Fastnet Lighthouse, standing alone in all its majesty far out into the Atlantic. The sun was shining once again and the whole countryside, the heather, the meadows, the corn-fields, the naked rocks, was glistening with moisture from the summer showers. I was filled with a great feeling of national pride when I saw the well-cultivated farms, the snug cottages, the look of prosperity in every field and garden, and when I thought what a different picture this same countryside presented to the traveller in the middle of the last century; a picture of death, pestilence, the screams of young innocent children dying in their thousands from starvation, and what a tremendous tribute it was to the unconquerable spirit of the Irish people that they survived at all. For that very stretch of countryside from Skibbereen to the Mizen was the worst hit area of all Ireland during the terrible Famine. It was a famine that need never had had such disastrous results—the virtual strangulation to death of four million helpless people in a few short years. Whether this was part of a sinister plan, to finally subdue a rebellious race who never ceased struggling for their freedom, is something so carefully covered up that it is never likely to be known. Hitler believed that the slaughter of millions of Jews was a 'final solution'. Stalin thought that the murder of three million Ukranians was also a 'final solution'. Did England believe that the elimination of four million Irish would be a 'final solution' too? Whatever the answer to that question is, one thing is certain, and that is that all three were proved wrong. The Jews survived, the Ukranians survived, the Irish survived and their executioners are gone. Hitler and his Nazis are no more. Stalin's memory is that of an outcast in Russia. England has lost her empire, in world affairs she no longer has influence, she has only an opinion, and in a few years Scotland and Wales will have their freedom and Great Britain will become little England that she started out as many centuries ago. Injustice and the brutality that goes with it never really wins in the end. This is one of the great lessons of history.

> *Immortal Caesar dead and turned to clay*
> *Might stop a hole to keep the wind away.*

To understand the Famine one has to understand the social mode and economic structure of Ireland in those days. Seventy percent of the inhabitants were small peasant farmers with large families who rented their meagre holdings at fairly exorbitant figures from English landlords, who for the most part, lived a high life of gambling, drinking and whoring in London. These gentlemen came by the lands in the first instance as part of the plunders and spoils of conquest. The average landlord's income from such rents would be thirty thousand pounds per annum—a sum equivalent to five hundred thousand pounds in present day money. The average diet for the small farmer consisted mainly of potatoes, milk and perhaps a little salted bacon once every two months, and his diet kept him and his family barely above the starvation line. So his little holding was organised to grow potatoes, pasture a cow or a few goats, feed one or two pigs, but all the time looming over him was the heavy rent. To meet this he planted a third of his arable holding with corn, and when this was harvested it met the landlord's bill. When the potato crop was struck by a disease unknown in those days it failed completely and the tubers rotted in the ground. The family was then deprived of their main food at one swoop, but they could have survived if they hadn't to hand over their corn for rent. Something like this happened in England when the potato crop failed and the English peasant was allowed to keep his corn and was therefore able to survive by substituting bread for potatoes. But not so in Ireland. While millions were dying of starvation on the roadside, hundreds of thousands of tons of corn were being exported to line the already overflowing pockets of the landlords. It is recorded that at the very worst period of the Famine a ship coming into an Irish port filled with food from some charitable organisation abroad would meet six ships going out laden with rich corn. The farmer's corn was for the most part forcibly seized by the landlords who also made this an excuse for evicting the entire family and levelling their little mud-walled cabin to the ground. One of the worst cases of this was at the village of Ballinglas where twenty families comprising of three hundred people were driven out of their homes by a detachment of the 22nd Highlanders and their houses levelled to the ground. It was a terrible scene, young and old screaming for mercy while their houses and furniture were burned to ashes. When they sought shelter in woods and ditches from the cold piercing March winds they were mercilessly sought out and driven off the landlord's property onto the public highway. This was only one of such incidents. No appeal to the London government was ever listened to. Lord Brougham said in the House of Lords: 'It was the landlord's right to do as he pleased. . . the tenants must be taught by the strong arm of the law that they had no power to oppose or resist'. That slimy toad, Lord Macaulay, supported him: 'How do you govern Ireland?' he asked. 'Not by love but by fear. . . by means of armed men and entrenched camps.' But to placate world opinion a famine relief fund was started to which the English government contributed fifty thousand pounds while at the same time they gave twenty million pounds to purchase the freedom of slaves in the colonies. That most uncouth and ignorant of monarchs, Queen Victoria, who at that time had a personal income of two million pounds per annum graciously condescended to donate one thousand pounds. The Sultan of Turkey appalled at the suffering in Ireland wished to send a first contribution of ten thousand pounds but he was prevailed upon not to do so by the British ambassador who felt that it would be unseemly for anyone to subscribe a figure in excess of that subscribed by Victoria. All this produced a situation so appalling that it is

128

hard to find words to describe it, and the beautiful landscape I was now looking at was the one that suffered most. The story of the Famine in West Cork is very well documented by several independent sources. In Skibbereen the situation was frightening. Mr Nicholas Cummins, an independent magistrate from Cork, wrote concerning that town: '. . . entered some of the hovels and the scenes which presented themselves were such as no tongue or pen can convey the slightest idea of. In the first, six famished and ghastly skeletons, to all appearances dead, were huddled in a corner on some filthy straw, their sole covering a ragged hare cloth, their wretched legs hanging about naked above the knees. I approached with horror, and found by a low moaning they were alive—four children, a woman and what had once been a man. In a few minutes I was surrounded by at least two hundred such phantoms, such frightful spectres as no words can describe. Their demoniac yells are still ringing in my ears. My clothes were nearly torn off in my endeavour to escape from the throng of pestilence around me, when my neckcloth was seized from behind by a grip which compelled me to turn. I found myself grasped by a woman with an infant just born in her arms and the remains of a filthy sack across her loins—the sole covering of herself and her baby. A mother, herself in fever, was seen the same day to drag out the corpse of her child, a girl about twelve, perfectly naked, and leave it half covered with stones. In another house the doctor found seven wretches lying on the floor, unable to move, under the same cloak. One of them had been dead many hours but the others were unable to move either themselves or the corpse.' An average of one hundred people a week died in Skibbereen alone under these conditions, while the landlords, mainly Lord Carbery and Sir William Beacher drew annual rents of fifty thousand pounds from the town alone. But it was the same everywhere Ballydehob, Schull, Goleen, Crookhaven. In Schull Commander Caffyn of the sloop *Scourge* was discharging a cargo of meal, a gift from the Quakers in Bristol. Later he wrote in a letter that three-quarters of the population of the parish, eighteen thousand in all, were skeletons, with swelling of limbs and diarrhoea. In one mud-cabin he saw a husband and wife, mere skeletons, in bed, the woman screaming for food, the man incapable of speaking. In another an old woman and her married daughter with three little children; the old woman was already dead but no one could be found strong enough to carry her away. He describes seeing a mass of bodies, half eaten by rats buried without coffins a few inches below the soil. 'Never in my life,' he wrote, 'have I seen such wholesale misery.'

I remember, many years ago, taking part in one of those excellent lecture tours organised by the Cork Historical and Archaeological Association. We had parked our cars on the roadside near Crookhaven and in a field by the road a scholarly lecturer was giving us a short talk on the Famine in West Cork. He told us of the kindness of some charitable association in England who at the height of the suffering fitted out a ship filled with corn and sent it to Crookhaven to relieve some of the hunger. They had no contacts there but they felt that by consigning the corn to the local magistrate, whom they believed to be a man of integrity, it would be distributed fairly; but they were wrong. The magistrate was a breeder of turkeys and had a prize flock of some hundred birds, and so kept the entire shipment of corn himself and fed it solely to his turkeys. One day a poor widow, whose husband and five children had starved to death and who herself was near to death's door, crawled on her hands and knees across the fields to the trough where the turkeys were feeding and began to lap up the corn with them. The magistrate saw her and rushed out in a towering rage with his horsewhip, and whipped the unfortunate creature to death. The lecturer pointed out to us the ruins of her cabin which still remains as a grim reminder of those terrible days.

In those years and their aftermath the population of Ireland was halved: from eight million to four million people but despite this terrible holocaust it was far from being a 'final solution'. Generation after generation rebelled again

130

and again, 1848, the Fenians, the Whiteboys, the I.R.B. and finally Sinn Féin, culminating in the Insurrection of 1916 and the ultimate defeat of the British forces in Ireland in the years that followed. It was a strange irony that it was the grandsons of many of those who starved to death during the Famine who became the core of the resistance fighters who so ignominiously defeated the cream of the British army in West Cork. I have spoken before of them and of one raid they made to capture much-needed arms and ammunition.

As I reached the lonely Fastnet Rock and Lighthouse I recalled another great raid. Let Liam Deasy tell the story which is to be found in his excellent book on the I.R.A. in West Cork called *Towards Ireland Free:*

'Ever since the time we first found ourselves in a position to come to close quarters with the enemy, we quickly realised that one of the most effective means of coping with enemy mechanical transport was the road mine. For the manufacture of such mines explosives were the first necessity. Intelligence reports confirmed the fact that for security reasons the British had stored large surplus quantities of explosive material in the light-house rather than in any of the mainland bases. . .

The June sun was going down in a ball of fire on the western horizon as Dan Leonard steered the small motor boat, the *Máire Cáit*, out of Cape Clear, swung her first north-west and then west into the dying sunset. As dusk deepened into darkness, the British destroyer that patrolled the coast from the Old Head of Kinsale to Bantry Bay appeared on the skyline and the intermittent sweep of her searchlights could be seen searching the sea and the coast. Veering off to keep out of the range of the probing beem, the *Máire Cáit* waited in silence and watched the destroyer circling Fastnet Rock and making for Mizen Head on her way to Bantry Bay. The raiding party knew that they would have two or three hours in which to accomplish their mission—if no alarm was raised—and without further delay they now headed straight for their objective. Shortly after midnight the boat approached Fastnet Rock. The sea had become choppy under a rising wind which caused the waters of the swell around the rock to rise and fall as much as six to eight feet. There was no landing pier. Instead there was a large rock in which was fixed an iron ring. The boat moved slowly in and dropped anchor. Poised on the prow of the heaving boat, John O'Regan with a rope tied around his waist balanced himself like an acrobat to the rise and fall of the boat, timing himself for the right moment to make the hazardous jump from the vessel to the slippery rock. In broad daylight this would have been a matter of grave risk, but in the darkness of the night it was so dangerous that only a very brave man would attempt it. At a given moment O'Regan jumped. His companions could not see whether he had made it or not as a wave of spray swept over the rock at the time he made his leap. But as the boat sank in the swell his companions saw him with his hands gripped round the ring. In a moment the boat was made fast and the others were landing. O'Regan made for the two-ton steel door of the lighthouse. Fortunately, it was not locked. He opened it and raced up the spiral staircase leading to the room where the lightkeeper was on duty. The lightkeeper put up no resistance and all danger of the alarm being raised was removed. As a precautionary measure the wireless set was dismantled. Then began the all-important work of loading boxes of gun-cotton into the boat below. Seventeen boxes of gun-cotton and three boxes of detonators and primers were loaded on to the *Máire Cáit* by means of the lighthouse derrick. Within an hour the boat was out at sea again and heading for Gun Point in Long Island sound. There Mick O'Donovan and the men of Leamcon Company were waiting to begin unloading the spoils. As the boat came ashore the boxes were landed and the whole consignment was safely dumped under a large heap of dry seaweed in O'Donovan's field near the beach. It was so well concealed that it escaped detection in the search that was carried out by the British Military the following day.'

And so these brave men went home to the simple routine of their daily lives in the knowledge that the valuable cargo was safe and ready for use against the lorries and transports of the Black-and-Tans.

As I rounded the Fastnet two of the lighthouse keepers waved to me and I waved back—this time fully clothed! The seas were high, as they always are in this turbulent spot, the wind had risen and the odd wave was breaking. One unusually large one broke into the cockpit and drenched poor Maxie who was sleeping peacefully on the floor. He quickly betook himself, with his tail between his legs, into the shelter of the cabin. As *Dualla* rose and sank in the great swell I thought of Thomas Davis's beautiful poem *The Boatman of Kinsale* written in the pre-dole era when men were men:

> *The wind that round the Fastnet sweeps*
> *Is not a whit more pure,*
> *The deer that up Knock Sheehy leaps*
> *Has not a foot more sure.*
> *Nor firmer hand, nor freer eye*
> *E'er faced an autumn gale.*
> *De Courcy's heart is not so high —*
> *The Boatman of Kinsale.*

The wind that round the Fastnet sweeps blows in all its fury and in all its gentleness along the entire coast from Cork to the Mizen Head, and makes itself known in no uncertain terms to every yachtsman, every fisherman, every mariner who sails these seas, and there are few among them who have not the healthiest respect for it. It is not to be dismissed lightly or taken for granted in any way and those foolish enough to do so can be taught a bitter lesson. The gods that rule the seas are no playthings for us mortals.

I now put *Dualla* round on the other tack and headed her straight for the white lighthouse that marks the entrance to Crookhaven. The gulls were swooping and dancing all around me. One, bolder than the others, landed on the guard-rail and surveyed me with cold beady eyes like those of a politician when you are trying to get him to tell the truth. A shoal of silver mackerel broke surface on the crests of the swirling waves; the sun was bursting forth in all its glory through the meandering tumbling clouds; the wind was rising, the canvas full and the sailing superb. I have cursed and sworn at the sea many times but today I loved it. I was now on the last leg of my journey. Tomorrow I would have to go back to the fume-filled city, to a desk in an office, and try to unravel the many senseless problems imposed on people who try to do an honest job of work, by what Hilaire Belloc called 'the servile state'. The wild solitude of the sea would become just a memory, smothered under a mass of manuscripts. Dermot Kennedy, and his friends from the Baltimore Sailing School, would sail *Dualla* back to Cork in a leisurely carefree way without me.

As my hearty little boat plunged her way through the heaving seas, and the blustering spray swept across her decks I began to ponder on what advice I would give to some friend who might seek my counsel on lone cruising on the south-west coast, so as *Dualla* tore through the water, and Maxie prudently slept in the cabin out of harm's way, I thought out a list of commandments, so to speak, which I would type and hand to him — in duplicate, I may say, in case he lost the original.

1. *Sail in a good boat.* This would seem to be self-evident, and indeed unnecessary advice but you would be surprised at how many people ignore it and go to sea in defective craft. Here you must make sure that she has no rotten timbers and that she is not leaking unduly. Most boats leak a little, but if you find that she makes so much water that you have to pump her out every hour or so, then proceed at once to the nearest harbour, search out the leak, and do not sail again until you have fixed it. Sea-cocks, water inlets, toilet pipes should be examined weekly. Many a boat has gone to the bottom because of a defective rubber joining on

one of these pipes. I want to emphasise this point very strongly, because if anything happens to your boat, if she should sink or partly sink, destroying your engine, you will have to face the possibility that your insurance company may try to repudiate your claim using a clause in the policy in which you guarantee that she is seaworthy. The word 'seaworthy' is capable of so many interpretations that it is fraught with danger. Some insurance companies, certainly not all, may as a matter of course, invoke this clause and put the onus on you to prove her seaworthiness. This could involve you in a protracted, unpleasant correspondence dragged out over many months. All the while the boat-yard will be effecting the repairs and will naturally be anxious for payment. It often happens that at this precise moment the insurance company comes forward with an offer which is only a fraction of the cost of the repairs and it is at this point, with bills mounting and with the fear in the back of your head that you may get nothing, that the danger arises of your making a fool of yourself, and accepting the offer. You should ease your panic and refuse. It is still not too late to do what you should have done after the first two or three weeks. Go to your solicitor, give them fourteen days to settle in full and if that is not met then issue a writ in excess of the full amount to cover such contingencies as price or wage increases, bank interest etc. You will find that this usually brings them to their senses. No insurance company wants the publicity of a court case from which the public might infer that they do not meet their obligations and so, apart from keeping your boat in a seaworthy condition, read the clauses in your policy, especially those relating to 'negligence' and as to who may sail the boat in your absence. You may have a surprise in store for you. Remember insurance people are the most charming you ever met the day you go in to pay your premium, but you may find a different kettle of fish the day you go in to present a claim. Do not forget the quotation from the scripture according to the poor: *The big print giveth; the small print taketh away.*

To this general advice on having a good boat I would add that my preference is for a timber boat. This may be an unreasonable prejudice but many years ago a friend of mine paid an enormous sum for the very best fibre-glass fishing rod on the market. One day whe he was quietly fishing a jet-fighter passed overhead at enormous speed. Suddenly the rod disintegrated totally into dust in his hands—into billions of particles of dust—he was left only with the rings, the line and the reel. Now my fears here may be totally irrational. It may be a million to one chance that this could ever happen to a fibre-glass boat, but I am not willing to take that chance. Anyway a timber boat is much more homely and friendly. However good fibre-glass boats are it is a fact that they have not yet stood the test of time. Wooden boats have—for thousands of years.

2. *Constantly check your rigging and equipment.* 'God's help is nearer than you think,' as the Gobán Saor said when he found the purse of money on the road. But you should not always depend on God's munificence especially when you have neglected your own responsibilities. It takes only a slight defect in one small nut, one shackle, one bottle-screw, one rope, to cause a major disaster on a sailing boat. Even though you may have ninety-nine items perfect if the hundredth is worn or weak then the others cannot be depended upon. A defective shroud can cause your mast to break in two and plunge headlong into the sea, maybe bringing yourself along with it. A spent link-pin can put your rudder into the water and leave your boat tossing for days perhaps, without any steering. A worn link on your anchor chain can put your boat on the shore and batter it to pieces while you are enjoying yourself in the harbour pub singing your heart out. I have seen stanchions and guard rails that looked perfect but when tested would not hold a bag of feathers. Believe me I know what I am talking about for many such things have happened to me at one time or another during my sailing days, and few of them were not caused by negligence. A cynical friend of mine

136

once suggested that the proper ensign for Irish yachtsmen to fly would be a flag showing a large harp with one string broken, and written underneath the words "Twill do!' But it won't do. Apart from a thorough inspection before launching, all rigging and equipment should be constantly examined and renewed at once if there is the slightest sign of strain or undue wear. It becomes a matter of life and death if life-jackets become ineffective. Every year I have found at least one of mine so bad that it sank on its own, without any human being to help it. Safety harness—so vital to the loner—will often be found to have rotten connections. And don't forget the engine! One of the great hazards today is the number of plastic bags floating around in the sea. One of these can easily block the water-inlet, the engine will then over-heat, ruin a bearing or perhaps destroy the crankshaft and you will be faced with a bill for hundreds of pounds not to say a few months immobility. The list is endless. So check everything as often as possible. It's too late to sharpen your sword when the drum beats for battle. All this advice is appropriate to the man with a crew of three or four experienced hands to help him. But for the loner, cruising the treacherous shores of Ireland, it is the difference between life and death.

3. *Trim your boat properly.* In the excitement of preparing for a cruise this is something that is often forgotten. When we are getting ready we stock up with all kinds of supplies, food, drink, bedding, diesel, water etc.—indeed very often too much of this is stowed in the aft part of the boat which can upset the balance very much and put her down by the stern to a degree that she will sail badly. Stow as much heavy material as possible forward—anchors, chains, ropes, tools, spare parts can be stowed just as easily in the foc'stle, and there's plenty of room under the floor-boards for the booze. On *Dualla* I have made a special kind of lashing on the fore-deck for spare cans of diesel which are quite heavy and can easily upset the balance. Anyway it's always better to stow diesel on the outside in case it spills. Inside it can

leave a nauseating smell which can hang around for months, apart from the fact that there are few things as unappetising as Irish Stew flavoured with diesel instead of red wine sauce. It is well worth spending a little time on this question of trim, by rowing out in the punt now and then until you are satisfied that she is on an even keel.

4. *There is no hurry. When God made time he made enough of it.* Perhaps at this point it might be no harm to distinguish three types of sailing activity. The first might be called *Passage Making*, which means that you've got to make the journey between X and Y in a given time, in order perhaps to deliver a boat, or to hand it over to another crew who are timed to arrive at Y on a certain date. This kind of operation is best left to those who deliver boats professionally. There is simply no enjoyment in it. You are pushing and driving onwards all the time with no rest or relief. The second type is *Yacht Racing* which is, of course, sheer lunacy. Racing is merely an extension of our daily stress into the realm of relaxation. Not satisfied with browbeating our fellow human beings in the fierce competition and tension of the world of business we feel compelled to extend this aggression into his moments of leisure. A very distinguished psychiatrist once told me that many men over twenty-one years of age who have a passion for racing suffer from deep rooted sexual problems. However I will not develop this theme, as he did for me, because if I do I won't have a friend left in Crosshaven, and God knows I have few enough as it is. Anyway didn't the great Freud himself admit that all psychoanalysis can do is to convert neurotic misery into normal unhappiness. The third form is *Cruising* and this is what yachts are made for and what yachting is all about. Cruising is the leisurely meandering along from harbour to harbour with no urgency to reach a fixed destination. Anybody with an ounce of common sense knows that when we get what we want in life we become tired of it and we want something new. The same temptation presents itself to one at sea for when we are out

we want to get into a harbour, and when we are in we are on edge to get out again and on to another harbour. You must resist this utter stupidity. Don't be in any hurry to get out to sea. In every harbour there is a whole world of enchantment to explore.

You can get into your punt and investigate the little creeks, inlets and coves that abound in every anchorage. There may be a mermaid pining in some magical cave who is waiting to bewitch you with her love and enchant you away to live forever in the Land of Everlasting Youth. There are always beautiful walks along the shores which invite you to share their solitude and listen to the singing of the birds and the murmur of the sea as the little wavelets gently wash the rocks and rattle down the pebbly beach again. And do not forget to visit the graveyard – there is one near every harbour. There is nothing better I know to put you in touch with the unreality of time and the reality of eternity. In the glorious loneliness that wafts like mist through the moss-covered headstones you will be reminded that you are mortal, that your feet are made of clay. You will be joining them sooner or later, maybe sooner than you think; so you might as well get to know them and make a few friends. You might need their help one day, and contrary to what most people think you cannot help them but they can help you a lot. *Is fearr focail sa cúirt ná púnt sa sparán.*

Sitting on an upturned fish box in a sheltered spot beside every quay wall you will almost certainly find a lonely old man, with a furrowed weather-beaten face, tired and weary after a lifetime at sea. Do talk to him and give him at least one glorious hour of companionship. Invite him on board your yacht and treat him to the best that your cellar has got. Believe me there is no greater cure for depression than the light in a rejected old man's eyes when he finds out there is somebody who cares about him. Let him talk away and tell you what life was like when he was a boy. He will repeat himself again and again but do not pretend to notice. What harm if he tells you a few lies. We, most of whose lives are a living lie, should not be too put out by a few straightforward ones. Do not be pompous or talk down to him. Do not cut the lark's throat to see what makes the song. Remember that he, too, is made in the image and likeness of God. Also remember that one day you will be old and maybe rejected. There is a terrible scene in Montaigne where a brat of a son gave his father a beating in the bedroom and then dragged him down the stairs by the hair of the head. When they reached half-way the old man cried out and pleaded: 'Stop here! Stop here! I stopped here when *I* dragged *my* father down the self-same stairs.' If ever you do feel like being pompous I can give you an infallible remedy. Buy a roll of toilet paper, put it on a table in front of you, and meditate for ten minutes every morning on its uses. I can promise you will be cured inside a week.

In every harbour there is a homely friendly pub, a place where nobody minds if you spit on the floor. Find it and you will be well rewarded. You might find yourself in the company of a matchmaker anxious to turn an honest penny and fix you up with a stuttering widow. But whatever you do don't forget to give her time enough to say 'N...n... n...no' if she has a mind to. But a word of warning. Don't stay too long in the pub. Ninety percent of the fatal accidents that happen in yachting happen between the quay wall and the yacht—men get so drunk that they can't row straight or see where they are going and sadly many end up in the public morgue.

So, as I have said at the beginning, take your time. Don't be in a hurry (except to leave the pub) and let every little harbour be your paradise for a day.

And now for my final piece of advice to the man who who wants to go sailing alone:

5. *Don't do it.* Remember I'm not asking you to do as I do; I'm only asking you to do as I say. When I began this cruise I had the rather unrealistic illusion that one would expect only from a teenager. After all my experience in life I should have known better. Long, long ago I heard the old

140

people, sitting around the fire, say: 'There's no fool like an old fool', and in my case time has proved them right. I thought that being companionless at sea and alone in the harbours I would work out some magic formula that would banish forever the senseless unease that tortured my restless soul. The simple fact is that I banished nothing. I solved nothing. Suffering is part and parcel of the daily life of every human being and it never lets up whether you are on sea or on land. It is like as if you drove a nail into a piece of timber, you can remove the nail but you cannot remove the hole. You may fill it up but it will never be the same again. The most consistent trait I have found in all human beings, including myself, is an irresistible urge to live in a point of time other than the present moment. We all have our escape hatches. Some take to drink, others to sex, others to drugs, others to power and still others to the whirlwind of senseless social activity and many even to spiritual activities. In my case I tried to escape through the solitude of the sea. But when all is over we end up in the same mess in which we started out. An old Irish poet once queried the wisdom of going on a pilgrimage to Rome as a solution to life's problems. 'Why?' he asked. 'The god you seek in Rome, you'll find at home.' But the cruise was not entirely fruitless. I learned that while you cannot solve suffering you can deal with it. Here Joseph Fabry's book *The Pursuit of Meaning* was a great help.

Man may be trapped but he is not without choice. He can decide to give up, feel sorry for himself, storm against an unchangeable situation, or he can ask himself what he can still do. Where a person is faced with a painful situation which cannot be altered he can find meaning in facing it bravely and with dignity... The story is told of Tristan Bernard, the French writer, who, together with his wife, was taken to the Drancy concentration camp by the Nazis. While they were marching in a column of despairing Jews, Bernard said to his wife, 'Up to now we have lived in fear; from now on we live in hope.' From

141

the depth of a situation of despair, he had reversed the entire outlook, not by changing the situation but by changing his attitude.

Hardly any of us will be asked to face the kind of suffering Bernard had to face, but in our own little tin-pot ways we have much to learn from him, and from the thousands of others who turned tragedy into triumph.

Cruising alone is full of unsuspected perils and dangers. Two young friends of mine, Judy and Brian Harrison who sailed in their boat *Faraway*, the same size as *Dualla*, from Australia to Indonesia, from there to South Africa, across to Bermuda and the U.S.A. and thence to Crookhaven told me that they would find it easier to cross the Atlantic twice than to cruise around Ireland. Out at sea, once you keep clear of the shipping lanes so as not to be run down at night, there are comparatively few hazards. The boat will ride out the most violent storm so long as she had enough sea-room to drift, and is far enough off the land to prevent her being dashed to pieces against a rocky shore. On the other hand the risks involved in coastal cruising are many.

There are tidal races where one abnormal wave can sink you instantly. There are currents and cross-currents, freak winds, magnetic disturbances that may set your compass wild, submerged rocks, exposed harbours and a host of other dangers that can make survival in bad weather extremely difficult for a man on his own. Even in the wildest conditions, two or three people can work wonders with a boat and guide her safely to port where the loner would fail. So take a companion along with you to share the work and to share the joys. And the joys are many. As you watch the beauty of the world express itself in sea, sky and shoreline that experience will become much more intense if you share it with another. It can sometimes be very empty when you are alone. Why not take your wife along with you? I know you will answer me and say she does not like sailing. But are you really sure? Have you tried hard enough? There is nothing can bring a glow of happiness to a woman more that the feeling that she is loved and wanted. Away from the cares of children and home, out on the deep blue sea, the young love you felt for her long ago can reawaken and all the lost tenderness of the past come to the surface once again. Why not try it?

So there you have my words of wisdom and advice. God gives us wisdom, but we ourselves must pluck up the courage to use it. Off you go, and good sailing!

As I came nearer to Crookhaven I noticed the wind had freshened considerably and the waves were no longer in a playful mood. They had become higher and stronger and more menacing. The odd one broke right across *Dualla's* decks and half-filled her cockpit, but as it is self-draining I did not have to use the pump. It was now clear that I had too much canvass on her but as I was nearing journey's end it was not worthwhile taking in a reef. Instead I slackened the sails and spilled the wind. The sky away to the west was piled high with dark threatening clouds coming up from the horizon and moving steadily towards the land. The beauty of the forenoon was gone. The glass had dropped suddenly and dramatically. It had all the signs of a wild night. I got the evening shipping forecast and it gave gale force Westerly winds, seven to eight, as imminent in Fastnet. I was glad to be moving into the comfort of a safe harbour and when I cleared the Alderman Rocks I started the engine and turned *Dualla* into the long inlet leading to Crookhaven. I dropped all sails quickly and motored her up to the anchorage just off the village pier. Although there was only one-and-a-half fathoms of water there I let out fourteen fathoms of chain. This would give the anchor a solid grip on the bottom with little danger of dragging, and as an extra precaution I rowed out in the punt and dropped a second anchor also with fourteen fathoms of rope and chain. *Dualla* was now absolutely secure. I then took every possible precaution against accidents during the night. I stowed all sails properly, tied all halliards and ropes with strong lashings so that they would not make too much noise banging against the

143

mast, and I fastened down every moveable object on deck. This is a necessary precaution because such things as buckets, containers, deck scrubbers are easily swept overboard in a blow. Satisfied that everything was in order I sat in the cockpit, helped myself to a flagon of wine, and surveyed the little harbour and village while waiting for the long overdue dinner to cook. Maxie, sensing that all danger was past, came out of the cabin and sat beside me on the seat, sniffing the air like an old sea-dog from the Spanish Main.

After a good meal I took a short nap and did not waken until it was almost dark. I rowed across to the village and went into one of the pubs of character for which Crook-haven is justly famous. It was crowded and there were two or three different concerts in progress in various parts of the bar. I found a berth for myself near a group of English yachtsmen who told me that they had sailed over from the south of England and were making a longer cruise up the west coast of Ireland. They hoped to get to the Blasket Island because they would like to see all the places described by Tomás Ó Criomhthain in his classic *The Islandman*. Yachtsmen, whatever their race or nationality make friends very quickly and in less than half-an-hour we were buying drinks for each other and chatting as if we were old comrades from childhood days. There is one thing I have found out about English visitors to Ireland and that is the very simple truth that they are basically a decent, friendly and kind people. More than anything else they enjoy and appreciate the friendship which is extended to them over here by the ordinary people they meet. Very often they are amazed to find no animosity, because they have been partly conditioned by a lying media to believe that we are a lot of savages waiting for an opportunity to cut their throats. Sometimes it may be necessary to explain that the many slogans such as 'Brits Out' painted on the walls near public highways are directed at the excesses of the British army in the North and not at the ordinary English visitor. In so far as my knowledge goes the people of Ireland have nothing but the warmest feelings towards them. Where there is animosity it is directed at the inhumanity of the ruling classes. In every country there is such a small group at the top: politicians, unscrupulous industrialists and trade unionists, police and army officers, higher civil servants, speculators and their ilk, who manipulate the millions and sow the seeds of hatred between men. It was the ruling classes, and not the people of England, who were responsible for the holocaust of the Famine times. Indeed the average Englishman gave generously to every famine relief fund and tried in any way possible to relieve this terrible distress. It was Lloyd George, Sir Henry Wilson and others like them that sent the hated Black-and-Tans on their rampage of murder, loot and pillage here, and the ordinary people of England were horrified and shocked when they found out what was being done in their name.

My new acquaintances whimsically told me how fascinated they were listening to rebel songs, and indeed one of their party had learned many of them off by heart. It only took a little gentle pressure to get him to sing *We're off to Dublin in the Green* to an audience who listened enraptured to the rendering of this militant ballad in a strange Cockney accent. When he finished the crowd would not take no for an answer and he had to sing two more, *Kevin Barry* and *The Boys of Kilmichael* before they were satisfied. Not to be outdone a West Cork farmer jumped up on a porter barrel and sang that famous English ballad *On Ilka Moor Ba' Tat*, but when he was called for an encore he could only conjure up *A Bicycle Made for Two*. However he gave a slightly different rendering by omitting all reference to the bicycle:

> *Daisy, Daisy, give me your answer, do*
> *I'm half crazy, all for the love of you,*
> *It won't be a stylish marriage,*
> *We can't afford a carriage,*
> *But you'll look sweet*
> *Between the sheets*
> *Of a feather-bed made for two!*

145

One of the party of Englishmen was an historian and he was quite eloquently despondent about the future of his country.

'I have fully accepted "The Little England" theory,' he said. 'And it is about time it happened. What right have we to dominate Scotland, Wales or Ireland, or any other country for that matter? We have behind us a terrible record of slaughter and exploitation which simply got us nowhere, but gave us a bad name all over the world. In Kenya alone we slaughtered twelve thousand blacks in one year as against sixty English lives lost and what was it all for? Nothing! In the North of Ireland we have caused the deaths of over one thousand Irishmen and for what? To keep all the goodies and all the money in the pockets of a small bigoted sect. We lost in Aden, we lost in Kenya, and we will certainly lose in Northern Ireland. Our only contribution to these nations has been the landscaping of the countryside with graves. I do quite a bit of international sailing and I can recall the time when the British ensign flying on the stern of our yacht was treated with some respect. Now, when it is not ignored, it is treated with contempt. So the sooner we become "Little England" and forget about international domination the better. All I hope for is that it is not too late. England today is under the domination of the most diabolical disease since the Black Death, namely the abuse of Trade Unionism. In the old days the unions worked for the removal of injustices, insecurity, fear, and the improvement of wages and living standards. All that has long since been achieved and they are now drunk with power. The English unions are dominated completely by a tiny number of leftists, totally unrepresentative of the ordinary members. These people have set out to destroy all democracy and bring us fully into an Eastern European society of slavery. So far they have been quite successful. They are steadily getting various industries nationalised so that the bulk of industry will be run by the state and the workers will be terrified to vote against their masters in case they lose their jobs. They have succeeded in getting defence cuts of some thousands of

146

millions of pounds so that in a few years there will be no British army to resist any threat from the East. They have already imposed a censorship of the worst kind on the Press by calling it "worker participation". They are now moving into T.V. They have introduced restrictive practices into industry so that the average British worker turns out less than half of that turned out in other countries. This is called "employee protection". Terrorism and violence is called "peaceful picketing". Successive governments led by those two jelly-fish Wilson and Callaghan have been too afraid to deal effectively with these abuses lest they lose votes. Heath tried to put a stop to it but was defeated. I am afraid that unless some miracle happens the England that we all love will cease to exist, and will become another Slave Camp. Anyway to hell with it all. We are on our holidays and we may as well enjoy the little freedom we have left. So drink up, my friend—maybe when it gets too bad we'll all come over to Ireland and settle down here.'

'Be careful,' I answered. 'There used to be a slogan in days gone by called "Remember Limerick". You may be jumping from the frying-pan into the fire.'

The singing, jollification and noise continued but the time slipped by all too quickly until closing time came around and the pub emptied reluctantly. Outside the crowd broke up into groups, one putting the finishing touches to a concert, another concluding an argument, yet another younger group whispering words of love to each other, and would so continue until sobriety instilled a little common sense and all would go to their homes.

The wind was now blowing hard and it would be difficult to row out against the waves, but my English friends hailed me, and as they had an outboard engine and a larger punt than mine they very kindly gave me a tow upstream into the wind so that I was able to fall slowly back on *Dualla* and get aboard. I was now very glad that I had finished all my little jobs earlier for I was in no fit condition to balance myself in the dark on an unsteady and heaving deck. I got into the cabin, followed closely by Maxie, lit the little oil-lamp, got ready for bed, and despite the storm, looked forward to a good night of sleep, that wonderful gift of God that soothes away the cares and sorrows of life.

The wind was howling and moaning outside. It moaned and sighed as if it were some lost soul seeking admittance. There was not a star in the sky. It was one of those nights when terror stalks abroad, when 'churchyards yawn and graves yield up their dead'. Maxie was shivering and he coiled himself up at the foot of my bed and looked at me with a strange uncertainty in his eyes. The light from the oil lamp was weak and unsteady. It flickered and fluttered uneasily throwing weird and moving shadows right around the cabin.

I was just about to lie down when I noticed a stranger sitting on the opposite bunk across the table from me. I was mystified since I had invited no one on board nor could I understand how he got there. I looked very closely at him. He was tall, with dark hair parted at the side, a handsome face and dressed in a navy-blue polo-neck jumper. He looked familiar and I knew I had met him before—but where I could not remember. He sat in an easy relaxed kind of a way as if he owned the boat himself, but a frozen tension gripped me and possessed my whole being when I noticed that I could see through him onto the shelves and presses behind his back. Stunned is the only word I can use — stunned, incapable of movement. He seemed to notice my state of fear, and as if to ease me he smiled an ever so gentle and reassuring smile across the table. Where had I seen that smile before? I felt old and weary and tired in his youthful presence.

'Do not be in the least bit afraid,' he said. 'I will do you no harm.'

His voice was soft, gentle, soothing. Almost as if by magic my fears left me and in some strange way I came to realise that he was my friend—indeed perhaps an old friend. I became a little bolder. 'You are from another world?' I asked.

'Not really another world,' he corrected me. 'There is

148

only one vast universe of which this earth is an insignificant speck, isolated on its own. I come from outside, from outside time and space where only infinity reigns. I have been waiting a long time to meet you, but I can only stay a few short minutes of your time. I nearly met you twice before —that day in Dualla graveyard when they laid her to rest— and that beautiful summer's evening a few months later standing on the wild cliffs of Moher when you nearly put an end to it all. But you evaded me, evaded me by seeking an unhealthy refuge in the insanity of all those longs years since.'

'I really cannot understand what you are saying,' I said bewildered. 'My mind is not as alert as when I was young like you. Please explain what you mean, slowly. Are you saying that I am insane?'

'Yes,' he answered. 'You have been insane with self-pity for more than six years. You have failed to come to grips with suffering. You have failed to realise that suffering is an integral part of life, so integral that if there were no suffering all living would stop. Can you imagine what this earth would be like if nobody, and I mean nobody, suffered from hunger, or cold, or tiredness. Life would just stop still. It is these things that make man work to eat, to clothe himself, to build houses and to live his daily life. On a larger canvas everything great has its origins in suffering. The great idealists freed their countries through suffering, all great music was born in pain. The agony of the great painter can be seen in the galleries of the world. From the tortured soul of writers came the worlds masterpieces of literature. I think that only now you have begun to understand this simple reality. Sometimes your mind has been so blinded by self-pity and self-love that you could not see the obvious. As you came round the Fastnet, I seemed to detect that link by link you were breaking the chains that fettered you to yourself; the icy coat-of-mail which you had frozen as a protection against love began to melt; the edifice of your own mediocrity started to crumble. You seem to have learned one of the most profound principles of life: *there*

*can be no complete love in a world dominated by suffering,
yet you must expose yourself daily and hourly to suffering
in order to find the fulfilment of love.* So you see, the
cruise was not a failure after all. You are ready now,' he
added with a smile.

The fear began to creep back again. Did I detect a note
of warning in his soft voice?

'Ready for what?' I asked. 'Do you mean ready for
death?'

'You know, I find it very hard to understand why you
human beings have such a terror of death,' he said slowly.
'Dying can sometimes be painful, but death, never. Death
is the highest, greatest, most fulfilling point of life. It is far
more stimulating than birth. You know yourself that man's
daily life is a mass of contradictions, of unfulfilled hopes,
of disappointments, of yearnings and longings that are
never realised. At any given moment he is fed up and disillusioned with himself. In his youth life holds out a thousand glittering promises and long before he gets old he sees
that not one of them will ever come to anything. He spends
his days searching into a future for the realisation of his
dreams, for a realisation of that which never comes, and on
and on he goes deeper and deeper into the quicksands of
misery. All this painful trauma ends with death. When a
man dies he shuffles off every material care, want and wish,
and he gets rid, at one stroke, of the cause of all his unhappiness, his body. It is like standing under a cataract of
pure, clear, spring water after a lifetime of groping through
sewers. His soul now stands on its own, in all its glory and
power, invulnerable against the slings and arrows of time.
You have often quoted Frankl's philosophy that man's
ultimate goal is Meaning, but I think he should have gone
further than that and said that man's ultimate goal is to
find the fullness and totality of himself. Only in death can
that be found. Do you remember the last sad moments as
you stood by Mary's bedside when she was unconscious and
dying? Do you recall how she kept waving her hands outwards through the air as if to fend off some intruder? You

150

were that intruder. She was then beginning to experience the first beautiful moments of death, and she did not want any human being, not even you, near her. It is the same with all dying people. From the moment they experience the first peaceful waves of death they want to be alone. They want to end forever any contact with the earth, and the people in it, and rush forward to their new life. Death is the most beautiful experience of all, but I know you will find that hard to understand, just as the child in its mother's womb could not make sense of a poem of Keats, a symphony by Beethoven or a landscape by Corot.'

I was beginning to see that although I had cruised in very deep waters I was now well beyond my depth in waters of a different kind, the dark bottomless ocean of human existence. Everything happening was outside my experience, but I was determined to push on, before my false courage deserted me.

'If death is as good as you say,' I asked him, 'what about the terrible moment after death when God sits in the Hall of Judgement and damns us forever for our sins?'

'That is another illusion that human beings have. God does not sit in judgement on anyone. He has never judged and never will. God only loves. After death you will face the severest of all judges—your own self. Yes. You will be your own judge, and the only mercy you will show yourself is the mercy you showed others during your life.'

I was now completely dazed. This contradicted everything I had been taught to believe. He saw my dilemma and puzzlement.

'Let me explain,' he said with a smile. 'Man is composed of a body and lives in a world of semi-darkness. In that gloomy confused world the spirit is totally incapable of understanding God or knowing what he is. That is why no one who lives can comprehend God and if you cannot understand him then you cannot make a choice for or against him while you live. It is only at the moment of death, when the spirit leaves the body, when it stands there in all its freedom, power and might, is it capable of making

151

a final choice for or against God. That choice is influenced by the life you have led. If your life has been powered by selfishness, egoism, self-love, cruelty to man or beast then the spirit is so blinded that it cannot see God, and it can only contemplate its own nothingness and it chooses that negation of being which is Hell. On the other hand a life lived for others, a life of unselfishness, of tenderness and love towards everything, illuminates the spirit and it immediately recognises God, rushes forth into his arms and into Eternal Life which is Heaven. Prayers, religious ceremonies and other external manifestations at the hour of death are only the icing on the cake and they have little influence on the final outcome. They are part of a tradition and culture and are engaged in more for the edification of the living than for the help they can give the dead. In that terrible moment you will be on your own, beyond the help of any human being and totally dependent on the love you gave during your lifetime.'

'So there is a Heaven and Hell after all?' I queried.

'Of course there is,' he answered. 'Hell is a state where self-love reigns supreme, where everybody hates everybody else and expresses this hatred fully in every form that the darkened human spirit can devise. On earth people who love themselves inordinately, really hate everybody else but convention prevents them from expressing it. There is no convention beyond the grave and hatred gets full rein. Hell is the constant memory of lost opportunities. Heaven is the complete forgetfulness of human frailty. Heaven is a state where everybody loves everybody else with a totality of love, where all dreams and yearnings come true, where there is no pain or suffering or sorrow, only the beauty and magnificence of pure love. Mind you, if ever you get to Heaven and I'm not so sure that you will, you'll be surprised at who you'll meet there. A lot of the people you admired and cultivated on this earth will be absent. Heaven is not exactly overcrowded. There are very few popes, cardinals or bishops there, yet strangely enough quite a lot of priests and nuns. There are no politicians, speculators, striking

152

agitators, or people who inflict suffering on others for their own ends. No faceless ruling classes who inhumanly cause pain to innocent people. In Heaven you will find a strange assortment: unmarried mothers and battered wives, prostitutes and imbeciles, fools and cretins, cripples, the stupid and metally deranged, nurses in hospitals, the blind, the lame, the deaf—indeed all those who were to be seen in Christ's company on earth. They are all there in a state of perfect happiness and beauty.'

There was one terrible question forming itself in my mind as he spoke, and I was determined to get it out. With dry parched lips I asked:

'Will I see her again, ever?'

'You ask too many questions,' he answered gently. 'Anyway I must be going. I have only a moment of my allotted time left, but this I can tell you. She is there in all the beauty, peace and happiness that she yearned for during her days of suffering on this earth with you. Whether you will get there is very doubtful but I would not rule out all hope. Accidents can always happen. As I said before God is very fair. In good time before death he gives every man a second chance to mend his ways. He lets him see the man-he-might-have-been.'

As he stood up to go I was struck by two intriguing peculiarities. I could now see his hands clearly and I noticed that on the little finger of his right hand he wore a ring, the exact duplicate of the one I was wearing on my little finger —it was Mary's wedding ring which I had worn since her death. On his left hand, between the thumb and the forefinger there was a small brown mole—exactly as I had on my left hand. Where had I seen him before?

He was now about to step out into the cockpit when I plucked up courage to ask him yet another question.

'One more question,' I pleaded earnestly. 'Please. I beg of you—tell me *Who are you?*'

He looked down at me with a wonderful gentle compassionate smile.

'You should know me well,' he answered. 'I am the Man-You-Might-Have-Been.'

He was gone.

Suddenly the cabin was filled to capacity with people, shouting, singing, making music and creating a noise and uproar deafening to the ears. The farmer with the geranium in his buttonhole was trying to relieve himself up the mast still singing *Faith of our Fathers*. The matchmaker was sitting crosslegged on the table playing *The Girl I Left Behind Me* on a tin whistle. The tinker was crouched opposite him painting a portrait of Winston Churchill. The commercial traveller I met in Kinsale was enjoying himself in a corner with a naked woman on each knee, all three singing *Onward Christian Soldiers*. The stuttering widow was fighting the air with her bare arms in a frenzy of terror trying to get out the words 'S...s...s...stop! N...n...n...no.' The Madame Defarge from Sherkin was sharpening the blade of a hatchet smacking her lips with pleasure as she riveted her eyes on my neck. Queen Victoria was perched on the chart table picking her nose and breaking wind. Several of her famine victims, their gaunt bodies half-eaten by rats were screaming with terror as her red-coated soldiers whipped them to death. The stench was unbearable. The thunder of the brawling uproar was ear-splitting. I felt so old, weary, exhausted and frightened as if all the sins of my past life were weighing me down. A deep depression of spirit possessed me, a kind of a dark night of the soul. I closed my eyes not minding any more what happened. Even if this were Hell I no longer cared. Then suddenly there was a momentary flash of piercing excruciating pain and I found myself floating through soft velvety air towards a clear brightness in the distance. As I wafted along this ethereal path I could see my aged body getting younger and more beautiful. All depression began to leave me and I experienced the most wonderful sensations of tranquility. As I came out of the clouds I found myself facing a landscape of indescribable beauty. I was now walking along a rustic pathway by a sea that sparkled like a billion jewels. A thousand wayside flowers drooped their little heads and smiled at me with a loving warm welcome I had never experienced before. Lions, tigers and other wild animals came running up to lick my hands. The birds of the air landed on my head and shoulders twittering with joy as they playfully pecked my hair. I walked a long way enraptured with happiness. I never wanted to go back again to the hateful sorrow-laden earth I had just left. Death was really beautiful. I was beginning to forget everything in the past. In the distance I could hear voices with a hearing beyond my physical sense, voices calling out to me in a chorus of welcome, but I could not see anyone. I sat down under a leafy tree by a tumbling waterfall which gave forth the most bewitching music I have ever heard. I lay back on the soft spongy grass, closed my eyes and rested, my soul filled with an ecstasy beyond all telling.

How long I remained there I do not know for time seemed to have no existence in this wonderful land. I could still hear the voices coming closer, and then I thought I could hear hers: soft, gentle and melodious as I remembered it from days long, long ago. A tender touch began to caress my face, ever so tenderly, smooth, soft, furry caress. I slowly opened my eyes.

It was Maxie, rubbing his downy head against my face as he always did in the morning to tell me it was time to rise. The cabin was filled with sunlight. I jumped up and rubbed my eyes to make sure it was all real. I pulled back the hatch and looked out.

It was morning. The storm was over. Everything was so calm and peaceful that one could never imagine another gale. Crookhaven looked just the same. Here and there in the village the odd person was up and about in the morning sunlight. The English yacht had left. A few fishermen were in their half-open boats readying their nets before putting out to sea. The wind that round the Fastnet sweeps had modulated to a soft gentle air, and everything was full of calm and peace and rest. My cruise was over. The sun was shining in a clear blue, cloudless sky.

It was another lovely summer's day.

MORE INTERESTING BOOKS

THE SECRET PLACES
OF THE
BURREN

JOHN M. FEEHAN

John M. Feehan searches out the hidden corners of the Burren, those secluded places where time stands still and where nature speaks its secret language to the human spirit.

Although at times controversial, cutting through sham and pretence wherever he meets it, he writes with great charm, skill and sympathy, and with a deep love of the countryside and its people.

He sees the mystery, the beauty and the sense of wonder in ordinary things and brings each situation to life so that the reader feels almost physically present.

This is a most delightful Irish travel book that can be read again and again.

MY VILLAGE
MY WORLD

JOHN M. FEEHAN

This is a book that never palls or drags. It is boisterous and ribald and I am tempted to say that it is by far the funniest book I have ever read. It is also an accurate and revealing history of rural Ireland half a century ago and more. John M. Feehan writes beautifully throughout. I love this book.

From the Foreword by JOHN B. KEANE

My Village – My World is a fascinating account of ordinary people in the countryside. It depicts a way of life that took thousands of years to evolve and mature and was destroyed in a single generation. As John M. Feehan says 'Nobody famous ever came from our village. None of its inhabitants ever achieved great public acclaim ... The people of our village could be described in government statistics as unskilled. That would be a false description. They were all highly skilled, whether in constructing privies or making coffins, digging drains or cutting hedges, droving cattle or tending to stallions ... I do not want to paint a picture of an idyllic village like Goldsmith's phony one. We had our sinners as well as our saints ...'

THE SHOOTING OF MICHAEL COLLINS

MURDER OR ACCIDENT?

JOHN M. FEEHAN

Was Michael Collins killed by accident of war or was he ruthlessly murdered? Both of these possibilities are calmly and carefully examined by the author, who has rejected the traditional theory that he was killed as a result of a ricochet rifle bullet and leans towards the possibility that he was shot by a Mauser pistol.

When the first and second editions of this book appeared they sold out instantly and caused a newspaper controversy which lasted many months. This new updated and rewritten edition, incorporating new and rather startling information, is sure to arouse exceptional and absorbing interest in this baffling and bewildering mystery.